GUIDE TO COMPLETE THE FORM E

&

OVER 200 QUESTIONS ANSWERED
ON FINANCES IN DIVORCE

GUIDE TO COMPLETE THE FORM E & OVER 200 QUESTIONS ANSWERED ON FINANCES IN DIVORCE

Helping you to complete the Form E, with hints and tips on the financial aspects of Divorce

Vinay Tanna

Copyright © 2023 by Vinay Tanna

All rights reserved. No part of this book may be reproduced or used in any manner without written permission of the copyright owner except for the use of quotations in a book review. For more information, address: info@garner-hancock.co.uk

FIRST EDITION

This book is a guide and you should always seek legal advice on your particular situation. We recommend that you seek help from a solicitor who is member of Resolution.
www.Resolution.org.uk

ISBNs:
978-1-80227-727-2 (paperback)
978-1-80227-728-9 (eBook)

Contents

Introduction 1

What is a Form E? 3

Questions before you start proceedings 5

What factors do the court consider when deciding the finances? 13

How does the court consider property matters? 15

Tax and Divorce 19

Jewellery and gifts 21

Assets owned by others (parents and business partners) 25

Maintenance 27

If a spouse is trying to get rid of their assets or hide them,
what should I do? 31

Pre-nuptial agreement 35

Should I attempt Mediation? 39

General questions 41

Form E – Guide to completing Form E 49

Completing Form E 51

About the Author 149

Introduction

After 25 years of work in divorce law, I consider that one of the most important aspects of separation is the fair division of finances. One of the most important yet underestimated features of financial disclosure is Form E. I have found that clients rarely understand the full importance and the wider implications of completing this form with care. This is not the fault of the client as there is little material or education on this stage of divorce proceedings. This is why I have written this book as a guide to lay out simply and clearly all the nuances of Form E and the approach to the financial parts of the divorce, which will help not only the client but also the court by saving time and, of course, costs.

What is a Form E?

A Form E is a vital part of financial disclosure in divorce or separation proceedings, and it is key to maximising its potential in helping you get your fair share from the division of finances. The form is used as a starting point by the court to understand the financial states of each party. This means that it will demonstrate a clear financial picture in terms of needs and resources, and, therefore, it will determine the financial outcome of the separation.

Why should I read this book?

This book aims to answer the questions about the procedural difficulties of divorce proceedings, and anyone who is contemplating divorce, in mediation, or currently embroiled in proceedings, will stand to learn much from this guide. Even if you have a solicitor, it is difficult to know what to ask and what is relevant. Solicitors usually give this form to clients without really going through it beforehand. Acquired during my years of experience with this procedure, I have included the various 'tips and tricks' of approaching Form E, which will help you to put your case across effectively to the court.

How will this book help me?

This book will give you the right information you need to prepare for Form E so that the process is as smooth and stress-free as possible. This will ensure that you have the correct organisation of information relevant to the stages of the form, which will strengthen your application.

What help I can expect?

1. When it is appropriate, use the help of a solicitor, as this can become a costly service.
2. Explanation of how to use the expenses and outgoings schedule to clearly explain your day-to-day needs.
3. Advice on valuations.
4. What to do if your spouse refuses to co-operate and give full and frank disclosure.
5. The penalty and consequences of not being full and frank in your own disclosure. It is vital to be aware of this.
6. Directions on where to find the form online.
7. A glossary of legal terms, so that it is easy to understand and deal with the legal terminology of Form E.
8. Online resources and reference materials to further strengthen your use of this tool.

I hope you find this as useful as the various clients to whom I have previously drafted this, and without whose feedback this book would not have been possible.

Questions before you start proceedings

How do I start financial proceedings?

- Your divorce/judicial separation proceedings must have started before you can issue financial remedy proceedings, as the case number used for financial proceedings is the same. You start with Form A and a fee.
- Consider the alternatives to starting financial proceedings

How long do financial proceedings take?

From Form A to the final one-day hearing, you will likely be looking at between 12 and 18 months.

How many hearings are there?

In most cases, there are three hearings:

1. The First Appointment,
2. The Financial Dispute Resolution Appointment and,
3. The Final Trial.

However, there may be other hearings held, such as a maintenance pending suit, whilst the main hearing is being determined. If one party has failed to deal with directions for disclosure, hearings may be adjourned and relisted for another time.

Can you recommend a solicitor?

You should ensure the solicitor is experienced and is a member of Resolution.
A solicitor's practice which is not a member of Resolution can mean the other solicitors are not experts which is likely to protract matters. Resolution is an organisation of family lawyers dedicated to conducting good practice in family law in a less acrimonious way.

Whom should I inform when I am going through divorce proceedings?

- The Benefits Office, as it may affect Tax credits – are you getting the correct money?
- Child Benefit Office – payment to the correct parent.
- Banks/Building Societies – to avoid any difficulties with joint accounts.
- Credit Card companies if in joint names.
- Mortgage company if payment becomes irregular or from two accounts.
- Employers, as you will need to take time off to see solicitors and attend hearing dates.
- Accountant.
- IFA (to find out your mortgageability).
- See below for what you must do to prepare yourself for any divorce or separation proceedings.

How should I be preparing myself in relation to financial matters?

This is a list of things you should be doing in preparation for organising your finances for any divorce or separation.

a. Credit Health Report – what is this and how can it help me?

Before you can begin sorting out your finances from your ex-partner or spouse, you need to get a clear picture of where you stand.

The starting point is to find out your credit status. This will affect the amount you can borrow and also whether it will be easy to separate you from the financial connection with your partner or spouse.

1. Your credit report will list all of the accounts and debts in your name, their status, how much is outstanding and whether there are any late or missed payments.
2. Check to see what is against your address and inform these companies that you and your partner have separated and (if relevant) that you have changed address.
3. You should also ask them to put a notice of disassociation on your credit record so that it is clear you are no longer linked to your former spouse financially.
4. You can do this by contacting one of the credit reference agencies, e.g., Experian. This is the most famous one, but there are others like Equifax, Callcredit, and Noddle.

b. What should I do with Bank and Building Society accounts on divorce?

Once you have contacted one of the credit agencies listed above, it is important that you contact the companies listed so you can start to disassociate yourself financially from your ex-partner.

While this will remove any responsibility you have for the account, equally, if you do this, you won't have any access to the money or any ability to make payments from the account. Before you do this, you must discuss this with your spouse/partner and or your solicitors. If you have any joint savings, again, you must discuss this in advance to decide what must be done. In the interim, you can request the account be frozen, or make withdrawals only possible with joint signatures. This can be useful if you're concerned about your former partner withdrawing money without your knowledge or consent.

Note: Monies held in joint accounts belong to both parties. So, either party is entitled to take money without the permission of the other.

c. What should I say to the Mortgage Company?

Sharing a mortgage with your spouse needs to be handled with care.

Moving out – This should first be discussed with your solicitor. Moving out does not make a difference to your liability to your mortgage. You will be jointly responsible even if you no longer live there.

If your partner has moved out and you are remaining in the property, they will need to contact the mortgage company in order to change their address. Even in this scenario, it's worth contacting your lender to advise them of the situation. The difficulty may arise if one party stops paying the mortgage and the mortgage goes into arrears.

d. How should I deal with loans?

- You both continue to be liable in the case of a joint debt such as hire purchase or loans. Whatever you do, do not stop paying or stop an account which is servicing this loan, as your credit rating will be adversely affected. It is easy to say, "Why should I pay? It's not my debt," but this short-termist attitude will harm you in the long term. There are a number of avenues open to you to get your partner to continue paying, such as maintenance pending suit or simply reserving your right to claim back the money at the end of the case.

    Note: Notify the lender that you are going through a divorce as this may allow them to consider more sympathetically any breaches of the mortgage terms.

- If you have any joint loans, don't forget that you'll still be responsible for the debt after you have separated from your partner. Even if the loan was being paid back by your ex, you could still be liable for missed payments. This is called 'joint and several liabilities', so, if your former partner can't make the repayments, you are liable for the full amount.

The best thing to do, therefore, is to get rid of any joint loans. It's unlikely that your lender will agree to simply remove you from the loan, but it's worth trying. It may be necessary to refinance in order to get the debt into one name, so if the loan is the responsibility of your ex, they should apply for a new loan to replace the existing one.

This may not always be possible; after all, the reason you took out a joint loan in the first place may have been that your ex was unable to secure the loan in their sole name. In this case, you may need to liquidate any assets associated with the loan. For example, if the loan was to purchase a car, you could sell this to pay the loan back and clear the debt.

e. When should I update the electoral roll?

1. You'll need to do this if you've moved out as this is where you're registered to vote and banks check this when they look to lend to you.
2. You can register yourself at your new address by visiting www.gov.uk. Just make sure you have your National Insurance number handy.
3. Make sure you do this before applying for any new financial products as it could mean you would be refused credit, or it may make it more difficult for you to open a new savings account.

When should you contact utility companies?

1. Get in touch with your energy, broadband, TV, phone, water and insurance companies to explain what's happened and have your or your partner's name taken off the bills, or have them transferred solely to your ex so you're no longer responsible for paying them.
2. Your former partner may also need to agree to this but the company should be able to advise on the best course of action.

Should I amend my will and life insurance?

- If you have a will then you'll need to get this amended if you no longer wish to leave anything to your ex. You will also need to get any pension you have updated to this effect too.

- You should be able to update your pension by contacting the company that runs it.
- If your ex is named as a beneficiary on your life insurance, they will get the proceeds when you die unless you amend your policy.
- Although it's something that you hopefully won't have to worry about for a long time, it is certainly worth sorting out as soon as you separate, so contact your insurer to update your policy.

Should I close all joint accounts?

You should make arrangements that outgoings are all met from either a single or joint account, otherwise, your credit ratings may be affected, making it difficult to get future loans/mortgage.

Joint accounts of all types can cause problems, especially where the other party is not financially responsible. If you suspect they may take money for reasons other than the benefit of the family, then such accounts should be closed and the bank informed of the impending divorce.

Can I take money from the joint account?

Money in a joint account belongs to both account holders fully, so, you would be entitled to take money from a joint account. However, in any future court proceedings, you must account for what you did with the money.

Who else should I approach to obtain advice when I am dealing with the financial aspects of the divorce?

- Your accountant, about tax planning and raising money.
- IFA, to find out about your mortgage capacity.
- Pension provider or specialist.
- Counselling to make the adjustment easier. Do not underestimate such advice; it makes the whole process so much less painful.

Advice from family and friends. However, be careful to avoid relying on anecdotal advice – "In my divorce I got...."

Am I allowed to take my spouse's financial documents without them knowing?

No; be careful, as the following could be a criminal offence or could lead to civil penalties:

- Opening your spouse's mail.
- Bugging the telephone.
- Taking covert video recordings
- Opening letters or correspondence from your spouse's solicitors.
- Showing private documents to others, including the press, during the financial proceedings.

How do courts decide on finances?

How Do the Courts decide on what each spouse gets?

The starting point is Section 25 of the Matrimonial Causes Act 1973, which lists the issues the Courts take into account.
   Please see link.
   http://www.opsi.gov.uk/acts/acts1973/pdf/ukpga_19730018_en.pdf *(pages 8-10)*

How does the Court favour one party over the other?

It is not a matter of favouring one party; it is the court's job to fairly assess the needs and resources of both parties when dividing assets.

I want my divorce finances to be split 50:50, so why do we have to go to court?

Courts look at the needs of the parties and the resources available. There are always competing needs of the parties, the main one usually being housing. So, the Courts carefully weave a decision based on fairness but start with parity. They then look at whether they need to depart from equality to achieve a fair division of the matrimonial assets. They apply the Section 25 criteria set out below.

My spouse does not work or works part-time, and I am sure he/she can work longer or start work.

Again, the question of Potential Earning Capacity needs to be looked at. Your solicitor may ask for his/her CV or seek information from his/her employers as to promotion/increase in work hours. Your spouse has a positive duty to justify his/her position regarding work. However, whether your spouse should work more depends on such things as costs of child care, tax breaks, and practicality. Also, if your spouse is dividing their time between work and child care, then it may be unreasonable for the courts to consider their potential earning capacity to be higher on the basis that extra hours could be worked.

What factors do the court consider when deciding the finances?

My spouse has another partner; how does this affect the finances in my divorce?

This may have the following effects:

- This may reduce outgoings if they plan on living together or marrying.
- This has no effect on the paying part of Child Support as this is based on Child Maintenance.
- This information is required in the form which accompanies the Consent Order called the Statement of Information.
- It will impact the final financial agreement and will go towards showing your future needs.

I am the income beneficiary of a trust; will this income be protected from my spouse?

All income from all sources is taken into account. The specific terms of the trust would have to be considered and, in particular, if capital could be released as part of the trust.

If the trust was created to defeat the other spouse's matrimonial claims, then the court will assume you have that money at your disposal.

We have more debts than assets; how are these divided?

The same test in Section 25 of MCA 73 is applied. However, in this case, income capacity may be an important factor. Also, the debts may be scrutinised as to how they were incurred. If one party has frittered the money away then they may be personally liable and this can be discounted from the matrimonial pot.

My mother/father/in-law is living with us and is supported financially by myself. Will he/she be considered a dependent for the purposes of financial relief?

This depends on whether this person was living in the property prior to the marriage or moved in after the marriage. In the former case, they are likely to have a beneficial interest and would not entitle you specifically to extra finances from the divorce proceedings to maintain them. However, even in the latter case, where there is no beneficial interest, the courts are unlikely to award special finances to maintain the in-laws or parents.

How does the court look at expenses, particularly when dealing with my spouse's maintenance?

The courts look at reasonable expenses. In Appendix 2 is a comprehensive schedule which acts as a ready reckoner of all types of expenses which should be included. Please note; this is not meant to be a "wish list" but a regularly checked schedule based on what is being spent during the marriage, based on standards of living.

When courts consider such expenses as reasonable, note the following:

- What are the other spouse's needs? If these are similar, then it may be reasonable.
- What was enjoyed during the marriage?
- Look at bank and credit card statements to check actual expenditure. This is also a good way of catching out those who inflate expenses.

How does the court consider property matters?

House prices are changing, so how can I protect myself by getting the best financial deal?

Recent case law indicates that courts are aware of fluctuating house prices. You should get as accurate an assessment of your property as possible. If you believe that a simple appraisal from an estate agent does not take into account such things as damage to the property, subsidence, development opportunities or a particular feature of the property, then it may be advisable to get proper consideration from a surveyor expert in valuation.

Can I buy a house whilst all my divorce and financial proceedings are going on?

- Yes, there is nothing stopping you from doing this; it would not prejudice you in moving on with your life. However, you should be aware of the following:
- Your purchase will be scrutinised to ensure it meets your reasonable needs.
- You will need to show documents such as your mortgage application, and loans you applied for to show how much money you could raise, and where you got the deposit from.

Can I only pay half the mortgage as my spouse should be responsible?

The issue of paying the mortgage is not considered in isolation by the courts. The consideration of the courts is overall needs in terms of maintenance. So, you could make a claim for Maintenance Pending Suit or wait for the matter of maintenance to be dealt with in the final hearing. You should complete an income expenditure form which can be found in the Appendix.

I don't want the house to be sold yet and I want to wait until the prices go up more.

This is not always possible and courts are reluctant to wait indefinitely to sell as they are trying to achieve a clean capital break so that both parties can move on. So, if you are reluctant to sell, it will have to be agreed between you both. You can decide a trigger event to sell either based on price or on a certain period of time.

We can't afford to buy two houses from the sale proceeds of our Former Matrimonial Home.

This scenario is very common and so the courts prefer to go down a Mesher or Chargeback route. This simply postpones any sale until certain trigger events but may keep the overall percentage each party receives unaffected.

My spouse is not cooperating with the sale of the property.

You will need to enforce any consent order if you already have one and the finances have been dealt with. If you do not have a consent order then you will need to start divorce and financial proceedings first before any sale can be ordered.

I cannot continue living at the property. Can I move out, or will this affect my rights to the matrimonial home?

Assuming it is not a council house or rented, moving out should not dilute your interest, but check on a few things:

1. Who is to pay which outgoings; don't assume that if you move out you can stop paying the outgoings. This depends on the financial circumstances of the parties.
2. Inform the Local Authority so the council tax is reduced to a single person.
3. Inform all the utilities/mortgagees (lenders of money).
4. Inform your accountant, as he/she may want to consider changing the principal private residence.

I am the sole legal owner of the family home; can my spouse still get a share in the financial relief process?

All property, regardless of whose name it is under, will form part of the 'matrimonial pot'. In situations where a spouse owns a property in their sole name, the other spouse is entitled to place a restriction on the title. This will prevent the other spouse from selling or re-mortgaging the property.

Tax and Divorce

What happens to my benefits and Tax Credits?

If you and your ex received any benefits or tax credits, you'll need to contact HMRC to let them know about your change in situation because this is likely to affect your entitlement. If you are no longer living together, you'll be classed as separated for tax and benefit purposes and you may become entitled to new benefits and tax credits.

You can do this by calling the tax credit helpline on 0345 300 3900, or search Tax Credits but ensure you look at any site ending with Gov.uk for more information.

Should I inform the taxman?

1. Call your local council to talk to them about council tax if you've moved out. If you don't, you'll still be liable for the council tax at your old house.
2. They should be able to explain what to do in your situation. They may be able to send you statements too so that you know it's being paid.

Would I be liable for Capital Gains Tax on the sale of my former matrimonial property?

On your principal private residence, you will not be required to pay tax on any transfer. But take care; the tax man has a strange rule that CGT may be payable after one year of separation. So, take advice early to mitigate your tax position.

Be careful also on a long mesher order when the sale of the former matrimonial home is postponed and another property has been bought, as those gains may be liable to tax. You should seek tax advice from an accountant if there is any postponement of sale.

Am I liable for any tax on a buy-to-let to property in joint names?

The simple answer is yes. You are jointly liable and you will continue to be until transfer or until issuing of a consent order as to how the property will be split.

I have never paid any tax as my spouse deals with this - what do I do?

You will need to ensure your tax is up to date.

Contact the Tax authorities and explain the situation and ask them for any documents including any past tax returns filed.

Instruct an accountant if you think the tax may not have been paid or if there are many assets and joint properties.

In any form E, you will need to make the court aware of potential tax liabilities or let the court know that your spouse will need to produce all relevant documents.

Jewellery and gifts

How do Courts look at the jewellery brought into the marriage?

This depends on what the jewellery was to the marriage. I am referring here to the usual case concerning the wife's jewellery.

All the advice below is subject to the following:

- Factual evidence such as photographs or video of the wedding as to what was given.
- Expert valuation.
- Whether it is a conditional or unconditional gift. All gifts are regarded as unconditional and belong to the recipient and are not required to be returned.

Must my personal jewellery be included in the finances?

The most important point is that not all the jewellery is regarded as the wife's assets; they cannot be ignored just because they were a gift. Even the jewellery passed down from generation to generation must be added to the matrimonial pot.

Does jewellery that has been gifted need to be included?

Below is a list of jewellery types and whether they are considered outright gifts and/or non-returnable, or if they form part of the wife's assets.

Jewellery given at the engagement:
The engagement ring may be returnable as above.

Jewellery given at the wedding by my family	Belongs to the wife.
By my husband's family	Belongs to the wife.
The 'Mangalsutra' (Indian jewellery)	Belongs to the wife.
Religious pendants	Belongs to the wife.

> **Tip**
>
> To avoid costly and acrimonious disputes over jewellery, you could simply agree to a "swap", mutual return of all gifts. However, take care as this can lead to more complications of what was given, etc., and the process of the transfer is fraught with emotion. Better to keep what you have received.

What happens to the 'family sets' or dowry given upon marriage?

In the case of substantial dowries, such as a house, car or money (for example), these are treated as a gift to the receiving party and form a part of the matrimonial pot.

My wedding was very expensive; can the costs be reclaimed?

The costs of the wedding cannot be reclaimed.

Does it matter if gifts were given to my spouse before the marriage?

Engagement gifts are conditional because they rely on the presumption that the wedding will occur. Once the wedding has occurred, however, the condition has been met and the gifts are no longer conditional. They will now form part of the matrimonial pot.

What is to happen to the money/assets I brought into the marriage?

These are known as pre-marital assets. Courts usually take them into consideration if the marriage is short (usually under 6 years – this is a rule of thumb) and there are no children. Otherwise, they are difficult to ring-fence.

I want to take my heirlooms passed onto me in my family.

It could be possible to take specific items which you brought into the marriage, but they may be deducted from the money/assets you receive so the overall percentage is not affected.

Can I ask for the wedding ring back?

This is a gift; you cannot take it back.

Can I ask for my engagement ring back?

This may be possible as this could be seen as a conditional gift upon getting married.

What if I say a particular asset is a gift my spouse gave to me?

This will be based on evidence. If it is considered as a gift rather than an item brought for the marriage, then you could keep it.

What if we cannot decide who is to keep a certain item?

Then it may have to be sold and proceeds divided.

Assets owned by others (parents and business partners)

My spouse's assets are owned by the father of the spouse. Do I have a right to claim this?

The following factors will need to be determined:

- Complex trust law will need to be applied; constructive trust/resulting trust.
- What was intended at the time of marriage?
- Is the father simply holding the property for the husband?
- Tracing exercise of where the money came from.
- Are there any expressed trust deeds?
- What does it say on the title deeds?

Notoriously, these types of proceedings can be more complex and lengthy as the parents of the husband become interveners in the proceedings. This means three sets of solicitors and barristers and three times the costs.

I am the beneficiary of a trust. Does this need to be included in Form E?

Most definitely. The reason is that even if you only have benefit which is defined in the trust, this is something that is relevant and you can produce the trust deed to show the extent of any benefit.

I used to own a property with my parents but this has now been transferred back to them. Do I need to reveal this in Form E?

If you do not reveal this then it may still be raised by your spouse and they may accuse you of still having an interest in the property despite it being transferred back. They can raise the point that the transfer was contrived and took place to defeat your financial claim under the divorce.

Can I change my assets into someone else's name?

You can, but you would need to disclose the transfers and why you did this. Usually, courts will treat any such transfers as trying to avoid claims by a spouse so will ignore the transaction.

Maintenance

I want a clean break. Is this always possible?

If there are children involved, there will always be an element of maintenance either in the form of Child Maintenance or Spousal Maintenance (also known as periodical payments). Spousal maintenance can be nominal (as above). The courts always try and achieve a clean capital and pension break wherever possible.

How can I protect my maintenance? What if my spouse becomes ill, dies or becomes unemployed?

The court has no jurisdiction to order insurance like a term policy or critical illness policy but you could negotiate this in the agreement. However, you should think of alternatives such as the nomination of existing life policies, death in service, pensions, and even credit card insurance.

My spouse earns a lot of his money in cash, so how I can get the maintenance I am entitled to?

This is always very difficult. However, there are tell-tale signs such as standards of living not matching real incomes. A clever way of seeing what real earnings might be is to look at forms where most people try and inflate their incomes – like mortgage applications, loan applications etc.

My spouse pays me maintenance in cash or cheque, but he/she can be a little irregular.

Make sure that you agree as part of the order, or seek authorisation from the court, that such maintenance is paid by direct debit. If your spouse cancels the direct debit, he/she is automatically in breach of the order.

I don't want maintenance; I want the cash/lump sum/asset instead.

This is called capitalisation. You cannot capitalise child maintenance, but you can do so with periodic payments (spousal maintenance). Some spouses do not want to bother with chasing their spouse, whom they know will not keep up the payment, or that they need capital to house themselves, in which case capitalisation is a more effective solution.

I have a court order, but my spouse has stopped paying me maintenance. What can I do?

Various methods are open to you, but you should apply within a year of the arrears:

- Get him/her to Court to ask him questions about his financial circumstances. This is a good starting point if you do not know the current finances of your spouse.
- Charging order. Usually, a lump sum secured on a property.
- Third-party debt order; this freezes money in his/her bank account.
- Judgment Summons – commit souls to prison.
- Attachment of earnings – order for the spouse's employers to pay directly.

Can my spouse get maintenance forever?

This is known as a joint lives order and is getting rarer. The court needs to decide under all the factors of Section 25A (2) Matrimonial Causes Act 1973;

> "The court shall in particular consider whether it would be appropriate to require those payments to be made or secured only for such term as would in the opinion of the court be sufficient to enable the party in whose favour the order is made to adjust without **undue hardship** to the termination of his or her financial dependence on the other party." [emphasis added]

This order is not necessarily forever; it could be until remarriage or when he/she becomes self-sufficient. Moreover, often periodic payments could be capitalised. The long stop is the death of either party.

If there were to be maintenance, it would be for a short period until some trigger event such as the youngest child reaching 18 or leaving full-time education, or for a certain time to enable one party to obtain full-time secured employment.

If a spouse is trying to get rid of their assets or hide them, what should I do?

My spouse is hiding something; how can I discover what he/she has?

A good solicitor will be able to look at Form E and the financial documents which have been disclosed and spot a lot of tell-tale signs such as:

- Regular payments in or out.
- A large number of cash withdrawals which do not tally with general day-to-day expenditure (which should be cross-referenced with his schedule of outgoings or lifestyle).
- Payments to or from unknown recipient or recipients.
- Regular cash sums being withdrawn.
- Lifestyle which does not match income.
- Missing documents such as missing bank statements.
- A lot of accounts with monies being moved around a lot.
- Borrowing from or lending to friends and family.

This can all indicate that more investigation is required and questions need to be put to the spouse.

You can use a device called a 'questionnaire', which can be presented to your spouse during the proceedings, asking your spouse directly about suspicions you might have. However, the Judge can scrutinise such questions to avoid onerous or nonsense questions.

I am worried my spouse may try to hide money or assets – What should I do?

This is where your own knowledge of the family finances is very useful. Although you cannot make speculative requests for information from your spouse, it can be wide enough to cover most scenarios, i.e., you can ask for information on any dormant or closed accounts in the last 5 years. If you believe your spouse owns another property, you can ask for the court to order a PN1 search through the land registry. This will show any properties in your spouse's name. See our section on Adverse Inference. This is an effective way of showing to the court that your spouse has more assets than he/she is declaring.

I think my spouse is about to get rid of his assets – what can I do about it?

You should immediately seek help from a solicitor to obtain an "S37 order". This is similar to a freezing injunction, freezing any such transaction. However, this must be done quickly otherwise, it may be difficult to trace or recover assets.

What if Form E is not accurate?

The following could be the consequences of not having completed this carefully:

a. Correspondence between solicitors as to these or any alleged expenses and asking for documentary proof of such outgoings.
b. Formal Questionnaires which the court can ask you to answer.
c. The Court can infer "adverse inferences" – See our article on what this means. In short, adverse inferences are assumptions which can be made by the court at any trial where:
   i. The information provided by one party is not complete; or
   ii. Does not make sense; or
   iii. Does not tally with other documents provided by the parties; or
   iv. Is inconsistent with the lifestyle of the parties; or

v. The party failed to provide a proper and plausible explanation; and
vi. The party has been evasive in his/her answers;

g. The court can seek any information by placing a penal notice on any order for you to produce the information. If this is still not produced, you could be put into prison. See our article on Non-Disclosure.
h. You will be questioned on any parts of your Form E at the Trial. Your spouse's barrister could cross-examine you under oath
i. Not providing full and frank disclosure will mean that it could discredit some of your other disclosures. For example, you're less likely to be believed or your evidence relied upon at any trial and it could mean the Judge is more generous to your spouse because he feels that there simply has not been proper full and frank disclosure on your part.

What if my spouse does not give an accurate picture of her outgoings and future expense?

a. You can directly challenge the spouse in correspondence
b. Ask her formal questions and ask the court to order her to answer them
c. Challenge your spouse using your evidence.

This is very effective in cross-examination and could discredit the evidence of your spouse

Finally, this Schedule is key to effectively dealing with crucial issues on the division of the matrimonial finances. Getting it right now will save a lot of time and expense.

Pre-nuptial agreement

If I ever got married again, should I get a pre-nuptial agreement to protect me?

There is good and bad news. On the one hand, the bad news is that in England and Wales, pre-nuptial agreements are not enforceable on public policy grounds. The historic reason is to avoid unscrupulous husbands from taking advantage of their vulnerable wives.

On the other hand, the good news is that such agreements may be persuasive for the courts when seeing the intention of the parties in any future divorce and would be included as one of the factors to be considered by the courts under Section 25 of the Matrimonial Causes Act 1973. So, all is not lost.

Furthermore, if you start divorce proceedings in another country, then such documents could be used more effectively. In addition, it is hoped that in about 5 years, the law may recognise pre-nuptial agreements. There have been a number of cases recently where the pre-nuptial agreement has been legally recognised (Crossley v Crossley being the lead recent case). Also, the pre-nuptial agreement is recognised in many European jurisdictions, and it is only a matter of time before it will be adopted by the UK, given our involvement with the EU.

Does having children affect the pre-nuptial agreement?

Yes, the considerations in a pre-nuptial agreement will be the respective needs of the parties. As consenting adults, the parties are capable of agreeing to a settlement, however, once there are any children of the marriage, the court's primary concern will be their welfare. On divorce, the Court will override the terms of a pre-nuptial agreement in order to ensure that the children's needs are met, even if the parties agreed in the pre-nuptial that this would not be the case.

What types of things can I enter into a pre-nuptial agreement?

Division of joint assets, separation of assets belonging to one party before marriage and any choice items of property brought into the marriage. Also, any inheritance windfalls during marriage.

What can't go in a pre-nuptial agreement?

Who does the washing up! Seriously, such domestic matters should not be included if you have a child unless it has clearly been thought out and is reasonable.

What must I think about if I am considering a pre-nuptial?

This can be a very sensitive issue to discuss with your partner, so discuss it early. Some consider entering into a pre-nuptial as setting yourself up to fail and it is highly possible that you may be asked, "Why would we need a pre-nuptial if we are going to be together forever?" Unfortunately, this book cannot provide you with an answer to that question, nor the perfect way to ask your partner to enter into such an agreement. However, one possible way to consider the pre-nuptial agreement is to liken it to travel insurance – although you don't plan to get sick on holiday, you want to make sure you're protected if you do!

You can be diplomatic and say that you have heard about/had bad experiences of divorce. You need to protect assets which will go to your existing children. It is mutual protection. It will avoid any acrimony at the end. As with any relationship, you are approaching such matters directly so that they do not pose problems in the future.

- Both parties must have independent legal advice.
- There must be full and frank disclosure of each other's financial resources.
- Provision for children can be taken into account.
- Must be entered into at least 21 days before the wedding.

How would courts view such a pre-nuptial agreement?

They are one of the factors under Section 25 criteria that the court would look at.

Courts would look at how the pre-nuptial agreement came about; they may even look at the file of the solicitors who advised. So, keep a copy of the file as they are often destroyed after 6 years.

Courts would check if there had been proper disclosure including possible windfalls in the future.

Courts would apply the following test – "there would be no manifest injustice in holding the parties to the terms of their agreement" [K –v- K 2003 IFLR 120)

Can I specify a particular settlement to be given to my spouse upon a determining event, for example, "he/she gets nothing if they are adulterous"?

Unfortunately, the pre-nuptial agreement does not specifically cater for the way that the marriage has broken down. This particular question is given greater precedence in the US, as opposed to the jurisdiction of England and Wales.

Should I attempt Mediation?

- Mediation – www.mediation.org.uk – This is a very cheap and efficient way of going about dealing with our affairs. It involves a mediator who will help both of you try and resolve matters. Usually, both spouses will have solicitors – however, they do not actually attend this mediation but advise the respective parties.
- Settlement rates for those going through mediation are high.
- Even if an early attempt at non-lawyer mediation has not worked, mediation or a round table meeting with lawyers and clients can allow parties to explore possibilities of settlement and even an early evaluation of the case as the mediator is usually a senior family barrister with a lot of experience in dealing with matrimonial matters.
- You cannot proceed with financial proceedings (unless you have or are within one of the exemptions) unless you have tried mediation.

My spouse is not cooperating and does not wish to engage in mediation – what should I do?

You should still make the appointment with the mediator who will write to your spouse encouraging him/her to cooperate. If your spouse does not engage with the process then the mediator will issue you with a MIAM certificate which will allow you to proceed with court proceedings.

Should I stop mediation if my spouse is not revealing all his assets?

No, you should ask the mediator to assist you in persuading your spouse to be full and frank in his disclosure. You should then tell the mediator to reflect your suspicions of non-disclosure in the memorandum of understanding, which is a document produced by the mediator at the end of the mediation reflecting where you both stand in your finances.

General questions

I do not want a complicated document about our separation; I just want to confirm to the authorities that my husband and I are separated – What should I do?

You can do this by way of a Statutory Declaration; both of you can have one (mutual declarations) or one of you can have one.

These can be used for schools, grants, and other authorities.

My spouse has been diagnosed with a terminal disease. How will this affect divorce and finances?

This can be a complicated situation. You are better off being their spouse rather than an ex-spouse. You may be treated more generously in pensions and possibly tax.

If an illness is terminal with death anticipated within a year, then good financial advice needs to be obtained.

If there is uncertainty, this can be problematic and the courts could see your spouse's needs as possibly being greater. However, discussions on any untimely death and how the children will be looked after are of the utmost importance.

The issue which you need to think about is as follows:

- Asking questions about prognosis.
- Getting good independent legal and pension advice.
- Establishing exactly what the ill spouse will need in the best and worse scenarios.

Why do I have to pay 5p to my spouse?

This is known as Nominal Maintenance or 'leaving the door slightly open'. It is usually to protect the spouse with the child/children in case something unexpected happens in their lives which means they would need to go back to the court to ask for maintenance from the other spouse.

What is the chance my case will settle before the final trial?

Many cases do not ever go to final trial. This is because the whole financial remedy procedure is tailored for settlement. For example;

- All parties must negotiate before you commence financial proceedings.
- During the early hearings, FDA and FDR, the court encourages the parties to settle.
- For all hearings, parties must be at court at least one hour early so there is time for discussion between the parties' representatives.
- Offers of settlement are encouraged to be made early.
- Judges actively manage cases, giving valuable indications as to the types of orders they would make if they were trying the matter.
- Ask your solicitor about a realistic appraisal of the case.
- Instruct a barrister and obtain a second opinion.

Can my spouse claim on my estate after my death?

If the correct provision is set out in the final order under the Inheritance (Provision for Family and Dependants) Act 1975.

You should also check that you have made most of benefits lump sum benefits upon death.

> **Tip:**
>
> A tax tip is to have this sum "written in trust". This means that instead of it going straight to your estate (which your ex-spouse could claim), it is written in trust to a nominated person. This has a number of advantages:
>
> - To avoid Inheritance Tax (IHT), write the sum in trust for a nominated person.
> - Consider a Flexible Power of Attorney Trust (FPAT), which has the following advantages:
> - Pension fund held in trust (no IHT)
> - Income to nominated persons such as your children
> - Trustees can pay out capital to your ex-spouse or others

What happens if I am declared bankrupt during the divorce process?

The courts will carefully examine the facts surrounding how this situation came about. If the money was dissipated by your spouse or its use was not in your control, then your liability will be limited. Worse still, if the money was used to jeopardise your spouse's entitlement, then this too will be considered.

What happens to our pet on divorce?

The approach the Courts take is firstly to establish who normally keeps the animal and how it came about that the animal is with the couple; i.e., Was it brought into the marriage, effectively treated like a chattel?

Courts will consider whether the cost of keeping the animal can form part of the income needs of the parties and potentially, they can even be awarded maintenance for looking after the animal. All the circumstances relating to the animal will be considered, just like any other chattel. The final decision, noting all the circumstances, lies with the court and the animal is treated just as if it was a television set or a sofa.

If my spouse does not disclose that she or he is engaged to be married or indeed intends to get married, (different from a girlfriend/boyfriend situation), can I consent to a financial agreement or can I set it aside?

In the case of Livesey and Jenkins (1984), the House of Lords concluded that this was a valid disclosure which should have been made by the wife in this case who was engaged, but failed to notify her divorcing husband of this fact. However, the onus is on the party settling the matter to get as much financial information as possible and investigate it fully before settling this matter. Only in rare circumstances, where there is clear intention to hoodwink the other party and this is a material omission, would it make a difference to the overall settlement.

What is a mesher order?

This is an order made whereby one spouse postpones their claim until certain trigger events such as:

- When the other spouse gets married
- If the other spouse cohabits with another for more than 6 months
- The death of the spouse or the youngest child attaining maturity (reaching the age of 18) or leaving full-time education.
- These trigger events can be negotiated to include other events.

What does Without Prejudice mean?

Letters/documents marked thus cannot be shown to the judge at any final trial. However, usually, the words 'Without Prejudice Save as to Costs' are used. This means in some civil cases, (no longer in family courts so much), such letters can be shown to the trial judge, but only after judgment or final order has been obtained and only with regards to the question of costs. So, if you had made an offer that was reasonable and it was refused early on in the proceedings, then the courts could deem this unreasonable conduct and costs could be awarded against you or some other adverse costs order may be made.

What is an endowment policy?

This is a type of life insurance, and it is usually taken out with a mortgage. It has now become infamous as some policies have failed to pay out even the amount to cover the mortgage because the premiums were invested in shares, the price of which have fallen.

What is the real value of an Endowment?

Never accept the face values of endowments. They may be worth more than the surrender values, which are normally stated in Form E. Try to get a valuation through a TEP (Traded Endowment Policy), which is a market where people buy such policies as investments. You could get between 5% and 15% on top of the surrender value. The longer you paid the premiums, the more percentage uplift, as the first few years of payment are simply paid to the salesman as commission.

Cohabitation agreements – Are these like divorce orders?

Divorce law only applies to married couples and the equivalent civil partnership dissolution, which applies to same-sex couples, which means that cohabitees facing a relationship breakdown will have to resolve matters according to general legal principles.

What if I can't get an agreement with my partner?

If the parties cannot reach an amicable agreement between themselves, then the only recourse is to the law as governed by statute and precedent in the areas of contract, trusts and land ("common law"). However, before you do anything, you must attempt mediation or collaboration.

Common Law Husband/Wife – do they exist?

There is no such a thing as a "common law wife" and a "common law husband". We are just living together; nothing is in joint names – are we fine? It is not true that after a given period of time you automatically acquire the same rights from cohabitation as married or civilly partnered couples. Someone cannot claim a share in their partner's house even if they have paid bills or have had children together.

Can I apply for the Decree Absolute because the Petitioner spouse has not done so?

It is still up to the discretion of the Court whether to allow the Decree Nisi to be pronounced.

If the financial matters have been settled, then of course you can make an application in the standard application notice under Part 18 of the Family Proceeding Rules 2010. You can even ask for costs for doing so on the basis that the Petitioner has failed to make the application.

> **Tip:**
>
> To appease the other side when making an application for the Decree Nisi to be made absolute, you must give an undertaking that the Petitioner could still benefit under any pension on death in the same way they would have done if you were still spouses. Also, you must agree not to alter your domicile pending the resolution of the financial proceedings. This is to alleviate any concerns that the spouse may not be able to claim against the spouse's estate in the event of death. Provided the deceased spouse died within 12 months of the Decree Absolute, the Court has the discretion to treat the spouse as if they were still a spouse. However, it is unlikely that in normal cases proceedings could be completed within 12 months so the application would have to be made or an undertaking given.

Why can't I apply for the decree absolute when my finances are still to be decided?

The spouse that does not have their name on the property will lose the right to live there without a court order.

They will lose pension rights.

If a spouse dies during the proceeding, the surviving spouse would lose out.

Form E – Guide to completing Form E

Financial statement – For a financial order under the Matrimonial Causes Act 1973/Civil Partnership Act 2004

What is Section 25 of the Matrimonial Causes Act 1973? – What factors will be taken into account when the court considers the finances of the parties?

This is the most important piece of law for assessing the financial division of the parties.

A list is provided under Section 25, which is used by the judge as a ready reckoner, and it includes the following considerations:

- What are the income and potential income of the parties from all sources?
- What are the assets of the parties?
- What is the mortgageabilty of the parties (what can be raised by each party if they were to obtain a loan)?
- Any disabilities or health issues of the parties.
- Ages of the parties.
- How long have the parties been married?
- How many children and what are their ages?
- What are the needs of the children, e.g., school fees, special needs?
- What are the outgoings of the parties and are they reasonable?
- What is the lifestyle of the parties?
- Any windfalls during separation?

- Is there a pre-nuptial agreement?
- Should any pre-marital assets brought into the marriage be taken into account?
- What are the outgoings of the parties before separation and after divorce?
- Are there any debts which should be taken into account?

No one factor in the list set out in Section 25 is more important than another although the court must first consider the welfare of any child of the family less than 18 years of age. It is for the court to assess what weight it must give to each factor.

Which is the correct version of Form E?

Make sure you go to the government website ending with gov.uk. The form is called (as of January 2022): –
Form E: Financial statement for a financial order (Matrimonial Causes Act 1973/Civil Partnership Act 2004) / for financial relief after an overseas divorce, etc.

The form is in PDF and can be completed but make sure you save it or print it out and download it. You cannot save it on the website.

How long will it take to complete the Form?

You should give yourself about 4 to 6 weeks to start gathering the documents and information, about half a day to insert the information and then another half a day to collate the documents together in order and check them.

Why is the Form so long?

This is the document which will be seen by the judge and your spouse to assess your needs and resources, so it needs to be comprehensive to enable the court to determine the issues in this case which it must take into account under Section 25 of the Matrimonial Causes Act 1973.

Completing Form E

Where do I find the case number?

Details of the court and case number can be found on the divorce petition, e.g., FD20F00034.

Who is the Applicant and who is the Respondent?

If you apply for the financial part of the divorce, regardless of whether or not you are an applicant or respondent in the actual divorce proceedings, then you are referred to as the applicant. This is the same even if the applicant for finances is the respondent in the divorce. A more detailed explanation is below.

The date of the form – When do I need to submit this?

The date is when the form is signed. If you later need to amend the form, you should add "date amended", so it is clear when you initially signed Form E and then when you later amended it.

If you are completing Form E under a court timetable, ensure it is served on the other side and sent in advance to the court. If not, ensure it is exchanged with agreement from both parties on the time of sending it (financial exchange). Where and when to send Form E is noted at the end of this section.

Where it says "The parties are", what do I put here?

You should put the full names as they appear on the divorce petition. Note; if the name is incorrect on the divorce petition, ensure you put the corrected details here and explain the change at the back of the form or on a separate page.

Tick the appropriate box:
  Spouse – where you are married
  Civil Partner – if you have formed a civil partnership

You are:
  Petitioner – if you have commenced the financial proceedings (even if you are the respondent in the divorce).
  Applicant – If you have applied to have financial matters reviewed or assessed due to a change in circumstances.
  Respondent – If you have not issued the financial proceedings (even if you are the petitioner or commenced the divorce).

Summary

Applicant or respondent?

> |If you started the divorce and you started the financial application – you are the Petitioner in the divorce and the Applicant in the financial proceedings.

> If you started the divorce but you did not start the financial application – you are the Petitioner in the divorce and the Respondent in the financial proceedings

> If you did not start the divorce but you did start the financial application – you are the Respondent in the divorce and the Applicant in the financial proceedings.

If you did not start the divorce and you did not start the financial application – you are the Respondent in the divorce and the Respondent in the financial proceedings

What do these terms mean?

Dissolution – you mark this if there is a divorce

Nullity – only to be marked if you are in nullity proceedings

Judicial Separation – only mark this if you are not applying for divorce but a decree for judicial separation (this is very rare)

Financial relief application – you should mark this if you are applying to the court to have your finances determined.

If the question is not applicable, what should I write?

Where any box is not applicable, write 'N/A'. – do not leave it blank

Can I miss questions out?

This is the warning found on Form E:

You have a duty to the court to give a full, frank and clear disclosure of all your financial and other relevant circumstances. A failure to give full and accurate disclosure may result in any order the court makes being set aside. If you are found to have been deliberately untruthful, criminal proceedings may be brought against you for fraud under the Fraud Act 2006. The information given in this form must be confirmed by a statement of truth. Proceedings for contempt of court may be brought against a person who makes, or causes to be made, a false statement in a document verified by a statement of truth.

What if I do not know what to put in the form?

You must seek advice; this is not a reasonable excuse and the courts will not look favourably at incomplete forms.

If you do not have the information, say so and also include when you asked for the information and when you anticipate it coming.

What are the consequences of non-disclosure?

- Costs could be awarded against you
- There could be delays
- You could lose credibility and weaken your case
- Adverse inference could be drawn from your non-disclosure which means that the court will either assume you have the assets or deem that you are hiding assets or income
- You could be committed to prison or fined for fraud/contempt of court

How do I present the supporting information?

All supporting documents must be included in the form – A ring binder with tabs is a useful way of presenting the information. Each tab is referenced to a particular section in Form E.
Example:
    Tab 2.1 a – Valuation
    Tab 2.1 b – Mortgage Statement

You must attach documents to the form where they are specifically sought and you may attach other documents where it is necessary to explain or clarify any of the information that you have given. Essential documents that must accompany this statement are detailed in the form. If there is not enough room on the form for any particular piece of information, you may continue on an attached sheet of paper.

What do you put in 'Solicitor's Fee'?

Your solicitor will have a special account number. This will begin with PB. Leave blank if not using a solicitor and instead, write down 'litigant in person'.

This statement is filed by

What do I put here?

If you do not have a solicitor, simply say "Litigant in person".

Question 1.1 – Full name

What if my name has changed or I am not using my married name?
Please show both names and explain this on the supplementary sheet.

Question 1.4 Occupation

What if I am about to change occupation – what shall I put here?
The form should be correct at the time of signing. So, state your current job and on the supplementary sheet, you can state the details of the change in occupation.

What if I am about to be made redundant?
Again, state your current position and on the supplementary sheet, state when you will be made redundant and make sure you attach relevant information like consultation documents or a settlement agreement.

I have more than one job; how should I state this in the form?
You can simply list your job titles here.

Question 1.5 Date of the separation

What is the date of separation?
If 2 or 5-year separation or desertion then ensure the correct date of when you separated is stated even if you say 'in or around 2019'.

I am still living with my spouse; what do I state here?
You can tick the box if not applicable.

Question 1.6 Date of Decree Petition/Decree Nisi/Decree Absolute.

If the dates of decree nisi and absolute have not been pronounced, leave these blank.

What is the date of Petition for divorce? (1.6)
Look at the divorce petition and you will find it at the end of the document near the signature.

What is the date of decree nisi?
You will have received this from the court, whether you are the petitioner or the respondent. The date is not when you received it but a date specifically stated on the decree. If you have not received this, then leave it blank.

What is the decree absolute? (1.6)
It is the final stage of the divorce. If you have not yet received this, you will need to leave this blank.

Question 1.7 If you have subsequently married or formed a civil partnership, or will do so, state the date

What if I have got engaged but not yet married?
You will need to reveal this later in the form.

What if I have a wedding date but am not yet married?
You need to state the future date of your marriage

What if I have had a religious marriage but not a civil marriage?
You will need to reveal this here and explain further.

Question 1.8 Are you living with a new partner?

I am living with my partner only on weekends; does that count?
It has to be permanent and your mail would need to be received at the house in which you permanently reside.

Question 1.9 Do you intend to live with a new partner within the next six months?

What if I am not sure whether or not I will be going to live with my new partner; what should I say here?
You need to have made a decision to live with your partner, say, for example, you have made arrangements to move into your new partner's home or you have given notice to your landlord.

Question 1.10 Details of any children of the family

Details of the children – who does that include?
Even if they are not your biological children but you have treated them as your children you should include them.

It says with whom does the child live– what if we have shared arrangements? (1.10).
In circumstances where there is shared care then you can state this here. If the child lives predominantly with one parent, then say the child lives with the primary parent and then explain what levels of contact you have.

> **Tip:**
> This is a missed opportunity if you do not state what levels of contact you have with your children. A
> party has to demonstrate housing and other needs which could increase your overall award.

Question 1.11 Details of the state of health of yourself and the children if you think this should be taken into account.

How do I answer the health question? (1.11)
Health is a vital aspect of the case which needs to have sufficient detail. Include:

- Congenital condition (from birth or long-term) Any conditions for which you have prescription medication.
- Mental or physical conditions
- Reoccurring conditions
- Non-medical assistance such as counselling or alternative medical treatment used.
- Recent hospital visits
- Whether you are an out-patient
- Recent visit to the doctor and why
- Prescription medication

Do not include:
Stress of the proceedings if you have not been to the doctor.
Historical health issues if they are not currently an issue unless they are a recurring condition at any time.

If possible, include a GP letter detailing these conditions and list effects of the condition, i.e., impeded movement or concentration.

If the condition is unusual, then ensure you provide context such as Wikipedia pages.

Also, disclose side effects of medication, including drug company downloads, and a copy of medicine packaging.

1.12 Details of the present and proposed future educational arrangements for the children.

How do I approach the issue of schooling?

> Tip:
> This is an important question which is notoriously left out or includes very little information for the courts to make an informed decision about children's schooling, which has an important impact on needs.
> Present arrangements – name of school (state or private) – year of child and year of completion. Include proximity of school to house. You may include a map.
> Future – proposed schools, areas of schools, year of entry – private or state?

Question 1.13 Details of any child support maintenance calculation or any maintenance order or agreement made in respect of any children of the family. If no calculation, order or agreement has been made, give an estimate of the liability of the non-resident parent in respect of the children of the family under the Child Support Act 1991.1.14

What goes into the box dealing with maintenance for the children?

1. Maintenance calculation based on maintenance calculator. Find this at www.gov.uk/calculate-child-maintenance.
2. Is the maintenance which is being paid voluntarily or via court order?
3. If self-employed and you are trying to work out the child maintenance obligations, then use the highest estimate of income. Please note; it is a common error for self-employed people to underestimate income because their accountants have advised them to artificially deflate income to pay less tax. The Child Maintenance Service (CMS), previ-

ously the Child Support Agency (CSA), will look at the real income and lifestyle of the payer.

Question 1.14 If this application is to vary an order, attach a copy of the order and give details of the part that is to be varied and the changes sought. You may need to continue on a separate sheet.

What does it mean in box 1.4 about variation?
If you already have a financial order and you need to vary it either by way of maintenance or capital, then include the original order and insert details of this.

Question 1.15 Details of any other court cases between you and your spouse/civil partner, whether in relation to money, property, children or anything else.

Other court cases – What needs to go in here?
This will include injunctions, non-molestation orders and Children's Act proceedings. It also includes criminal proceedings such as domestic abuse.

Question 1.16 Your present residence and the occupants of it and on what terms you occupy it (e.g. tenant, owner-occupier).

Occupants: This will include lodgers, long-term guests and children.

Terms of Occupation: Owner-occupier, tenanted under an Assured Shorthold Tenancy, Lodgers agreement, so if you are with parents or friends on a short-term informal basis, this needs to be explained as it shows that you have rights of tenure.

Page 4

Section 2 – Financial Details

Part 1 Real Property (land and buildings) and Personal Assets

Question 2.1 Complete this section in respect of the family home (the last family home occupied by you and your spouse/civil partner) if it remains unsold.

Address: Full postal address

Land Registry Number: You should find this in your conveyancing papers, usually under something called the 'office copies', which is an extract of your title deeds. If you cannot find this, you can go to the land registry website and pay a few pounds to find out. Be careful if you google this – do not click on advertisements which are private companies offering this service and who charge exorbitant fees to obtain the details.

https://www.gov.uk/search-property-information-land-registry

Mortgage: All the mortgage information is found on the mortgage statement. You will need the mortgage number as it may be needed later in any future order.

Type of mortgage: Repayment, interest-only, step mortgage, offset mortgage.

Details of who owns the property and the extent of your legal and beneficial interest in it: The easy part is who owns it – this should be clear from the title register.

What is beneficial interest?
Those who are not named on the title register but who may have an interest. If you have a trust deed that is not registered. Anyone who put money into the property, anyone named on the mortgage but who is not named on the property.

How do I determine what interest the beneficial owner has?
This should be clear in any trust deed. If you do not have a trust deed or declaration of trust, then you may wish to insert a percentage that has been agreed between the parties. If you do not know, then say "interest not known". If that is the case, then this is the first thing the court will need to consider so it can determine what goes into the matrimonial pot.

If you consider that the legal ownership as recorded at the Land Registry does not reflect the true position, state why. – How do I answer this?
To answer this question, you would have to have said that there is a beneficial owner. This question is, for example, where one party holds the property for another. So, if your parents asked you to hold the property in your name but in actuality, the mortgage was paid by the parents and rents received went to them. You would show any proof like a trust deed or even a written document showing the arrangement.

Courts carefully consider this, and again, if it is the case that you have the legal ownership but do not have the beneficial interest, you need to explain this in detail on a separate page.

Also, if your spouse owns the property by virtue of marriage, you would have a beneficial interest in the property, then here you would put your interest as follows:

"The property is owned by my husband/wife but is to be considered as a matrimonial asset and accordingly, I own 50%".

If this is not correct and you believe you own more than 50%, then say why. Here, you would need good legal advice.

> **Tip:**
> Many parents consider transferring assets into their children's names to be a tax-efficient way of inheritance planning but it can cause considerable problems if a subsequent divorce ensues and the property is dragged into divorce proceedings. You should have a clear document showing how you hold the property.

Current market value.
You can use an internet-based valuation, but be careful as the prices quoted are usually on the top end.

Use an estate agent appraisal. There are two downsides to this – you may need to have a formal valuation later on and you will not be able to use this valuer. The estate agent appraisal, again, can be overvalued and could be more aspirational than realistic. You should also note that a valuation in a volatile market will need a wide margin valuation.

The best and truest value is from a surveyor. This is not recommended at this stage but you could have this valuation if, say, the property has a particular feature which needs expert valuation, such as development value.

Finally, you can use your own estimate.

If you are providing a third-party valuation, you must attach it to Form E.

> **Tip:**
> It is recommended at this stage simply to pitch a reasonable value and leave any formal valuation to the later stage of the proceedings when, no doubt, a proper valuation will have to be dealt with jointly.

Current balance of the mortgage:
This can be found on your mortgage statement. Even if this is not correct as of the date of Form E, it will be sufficient for the purposes of Form E.

You must attach the mortgage statement for each property (if there is more than one mortgage).

If a sale at this stage would result in penalties payable under the mortgage, state the amount

This is known as the Early Redemption Penalty (ERP) and will be found on the mortgage statement. These will include the scale of charges if the mortgage is redeemed early.

Estimate the costs of sale of the property

It is usual practice to estimate about 3% of the value of the property to reflect the following charges: Legal fees, estate agency fees and other incidental fees for selling. This sum is based on the gross value (the actual value of the property).

Total equity in the property (i.e. market value less outstanding mortgage(s), penalties if any and the costs of sale)

So, this is an exercise in arithmetic. Take away all the costs of sale and the mortgage from the market value of the property.

TOTAL value of your interest in the family home: Total A

You may think this is the same figure as the total equity above, but it may not be as your particular interest might be different. For example, if you hold the property with your parents but you have no beneficial interest, then this will be zero.

Question 2.2 Details of your interest in any other property, land or buildings. Complete one page for each property you have an interest in.

Here, you must detail any properties you have an interest in. This includes an interest that may not be worth anything as you might be holding it for another but you must include details in this section.

What if I own the property with my spouse?
Usually, to make things easier and simpler for the purpose of Form E, this is halved. Note that this is not what happens in actuality but rather the property is put in the matrimonial pot and then the courts divide it fairly.

What if you own/have an interest in more than one property?
You will have to complete a form for each property.

What if I think the property is mine and my spouse should not have an interest in it?
In long marriages, properties are placed in the matrimonial pot.

However, your position may be that you purchased this property before marriage (and it is a short marriage) and so all the equity should be yours.

Question 2.3 – Details of all personal bank, building society and National Savings accounts that you hold or have held at any time in the last twelve months and which are or were either in your own name or in which you have or have had any interest. This applies whether any such account is in credit or in debit. For joint accounts give your interest and the name of the other account holder. If the account is overdrawn, show a minus figure.

You will need to attach 12 months' bank statements for each account. The statements can be printed off from the computer.

A copy of any passbook must be included if this is the way the statements are shown.

Why am I asked to provide 12 months of statements?
This gives both parties and the court a chance to see if there have been any changes in your circumstances, allowing them to understand your lifestyle.

> **Tip:**
> Try and tally your expenses with your bank statements (or credit cards). It will look more convincing to the court that your needs have been drawn from a credible source.

What if my account has been closed?
If an account has been closed in the last 12 months, then you need a final closed account statement.

If you do not have statements or have applied for them, state when this was done and when you anticipate having them. A copy of the request for the statement should be included.

Do I need to include an account held abroad?
Yes. You must also do this with accounts held with international banking institutions.

I hold an account with another person – Do I need to include this?
If you hold an account with another, it is not an excuse that you need the other person's permission. The courts expect you to get hold of the statements at your own cost.

My bank /credit card statements are changing day to day; what should I put in the figures?
The figures should show those on the date of signing Form E.

Note that Form E is a snapshot picture of your finances as of the date of signing of your Form E.

What does it mean when it says total current value of your interest?
The account may be in someone else's name and your money may be held by them. This needs to be disclosed.

The account may be in your name but someone else who is not named in the account has an interest, for example, if you are holding money for another person.

The money in a joint account – who does it belong to?
Joint accounts, by their very nature, mean that you both have an interest in all the money. Hence, if I had an account with another person and I took the money out that would be absolutely fine unless there was a prior agreement or the monies were held in trust or ring-fenced for a specific purpose.

Question – 2.4 – Details of all investments, including shares, PEPs, ISAs, TESSAs, National Savings Investments (other than already shown above), bonds, stocks, unit trusts, investment trusts, gilts and other quoted securities that you hold or have an interest in. (Do not include dividend income as this will be dealt with separately later on.)

You will need the following:

1. Share certificate showing how many shares you own or latest dividend statement or
2. A current valuation from the internet – print out the page of the value of the shares, etc.
3. A current value of the PEPs, ISAs, etc., – this should be in the annual statement.

How do I get a valuation of my shares?
There is a daily valuation on the internet. Print out the valuation for that date and work out the value of the shares.

Question 2.5 – Details of all life insurance policies including endowment policies that you hold or have an interest in. Include those that do not have a surrender value. Complete one page for each policy.

If the policy is assigned, state in whose favour and the amount of charge. This means when the person dies, who will the money be paid to?

What is the Maturity date?
The maturity date of life policies would be on death. For endowment policies, there will be a maturity date when payment will be made.

How do I calculate a surrender value?
Life policies may not have a value but endowment policies may have a value. The value would be stated in any endowment statement. However, in reality,

such values on the open market, if sold, could be higher. So, for the purposes of Form E, a base value as declared on any statement should be sufficient.

If a policy includes life insurance, detail the amount of the insurance and the name of the person whose life is insured.

You need to state the amount of the insurance to be paid out on death. Name those whose lives are covered.

Question 2.6 Details of all monies that are OWED TO YOU. Do not include sums owed in director's or partnership accounts which should be included in section 2.11.

This is monies loaned formally or informally by you to others.

It can include short-term loans and cash loans. – Do not include any business loans as these are covered elsewhere.

Do I include money owed by my adult children?
Yes, you must include all monies loaned by you. However, you need to include details of anticipated repayment.
Include any evidence such as a loan agreement.

> **Tip:**
> If you believe that this may not be paid, please explain as any figures here would be treated as an asset.

Question 2.7 Details of all cash sums held in excess of £500. You must state where it is held and the currency it is held in.

This includes cash held by children.

Question 2.8 – Details of personal belongings individually worth more than £500.

You should include the car you drive unless it is leased. It would be helpful to have an internet valuation of a similar car/asset.
Note: these refer to <u>individual</u> items of furniture and contents.

> **Tip:**
> Note that most furniture, TVs and household items are not worth very much second-hand unless it is antique or has a particular value.

Do I put in valuations of collections, watches, ceramics, wine and jewellery items?

A general valuation of the total jewellery is sufficient. However, you will be asked later to specify the value of each item, so best this is done now. A formal valuation is not needed at this stage.

> **Tip:**
> Look at the valuation you have put in your insurance as this is a good indication of value, but be careful as this is usually an overestimate. It is used by spouses to show that the other spouse's jewellery is worth more. However, these issues are ironed out with formal valuations.

2 Financial Details Part 2 Capital: Liabilities and Capital Gains Tax

Question 2.9 – Details of any liabilities you have.

What not to include:
- Mortgages (as they have already been covered elsewhere in the form)
- Overdrawn bank accounts (again this should have been shown at 2.3)
- Monies owed to you as trade creditors in your business as this is also covered elsewhere

What to include:
- Loans received for legal fees
- Formal loans (for legal fees) – you need to include a copy of the agreement.
- Loans from friends and family – to ensure these are taken seriously by the court and not relegated to "soft loans", have a formal agreement with a repayment schedule. Please include any evidence.
- Each credit card including those with zero balances
- HP on cars, furniture and goods
- If it is a joint loan and there is a difference in how the liability is divided, make sure you explain this.
- Any employer loans for travel cards, etc.

Question 2.10 – If any Capital Gains Tax would be payable on the disposal now of any of your real property or personal assets, give your estimate of the tax liability.

This would be, for example, buy-to-let properties if you had to sell the asset. Take advice from an accountant on this. A letter from an accountant would assist and would help to increase your potential liability.

Please note any sale of Cryptocurrency would also attract CGT.

Do I take account of my yearly tax allowance on Capital Gains?
You should be looking for a worst-case scenario tax liability, but in practice, there are a lot of ways to reduce tax liability with tax savings strategies. You do not need to take account of your yearly capital gains allowance.

2 Financial Details Part 3 Capital: Business assets and directorships

Question – 2.11 Details of all your business interests. Complete one page for each business you have an interest in.

What you must attach to Form E:

Make sure you name all your directorships of all businesses even those which are dormant or struck off.

What financial information do I need to include for this section?

a. Copies of the business accounts for the last <u>two</u> financial years – if you have one previous year and draft accounts for the current one, that should be fine.
b. If you have only been trading for a short time then a letter from the accountant with some projections would be useful to the court.
c. If you have no trading history and it is a fledging business, then a business plan would be valuable.

Do I need to include a valuation of the business?
Not all businesses have any value. However, there may be some value even for sole traders. Speak to your accountant to provide a letter.
If it is an established business with assets, then again, a letter from an accountant stating approximate value would be sufficient at this stage.
Note: It is not essential to obtain a formal valuation at this stage.

If you are a partner or a shareholder, state the extent of your interest in the business (i.e. partnership share or the extent of your shareholding compared to the overall shares issued)
You should consider any shareholders or partnership agreement – this should be attached to Form E.

If you do not have any agreement, state your understanding as to what interest you have.

If any of the figures in the last accounts are not an accurate reflection of the current position, state why.
This is a question which is frequently skipped and is a missed opportunity to explain why last year's, or indeed, this year's accounts do not reflect how the business is expected to perform in the coming year(s).

You could include the following:

Anticipate change in profits:

1. General downturn in the business and the percentage of reduced profits you anticipate
2. Lost contracts or non-renewal of vital business
3. Economic factors
4. Extraordinary expenses which will affect profitability.

Anticipate change in asset value:

1. Check that there has not been any change in asset valuation.
2. Check when the last revaluation of assets occurred.
3. Are there any other factors which could have changed the valuation of assets?

You will need to give some estimates of how the profitability will be affected.

If you are to use these factors then you need to give details and evidence. Again, an accountant's letter would be useful.

Some words of warning – your spouse may seek expert evidence and even forensic evidence, which will add further costs to the litigation.

Total amount of any sums owed to you by the business by way of a director's loan account, partnership capital or current accounts or the like. Identify where these appear in the business accounts.

If you have a director's loan then this needs to be specifically highlighted. You should also state clearly if you intend to pay this back and when. You should note that a director's loan, if not paid back within 9 months, could have tax consequences but also the courts can treat this as additional income taken from the business. This is the same for partnerships.

If you have loaned money to the company then this should be seen as a liability and highlighted here.

Also, if you have a capital account and it is in credit, say it is goodwill that you have paid for, for the benefit of the company then this could be seen as an asset/income which can be drawn from.

You will need to speak to your lawyer and accountant about how best to approach this as can have consequences later on in the case.

Your estimate of the current value of your business interest. Explain briefly the basis upon which you have reached that figure

Any business has an inherent value but sole traders will have a nominal value, as they are the business. They may be able to sell some goodwill such as a client list and referrals.

Note: Businesses such as window cleaners and gardeners usually don't have a value for the business.

Other businesses may have a value based on assets, such as a development/property business; in this case, valuations of income and property values would be important.

Other businesses will need to be formally valued and an accountant can help. Factors such as what you paid for the business, the value of a like-for-like business and profit multipliers could be used. However, each business and the industry in which it trades is treated differently. Your spouse will try and give an overvaluation and may use different ways of calculating value. You need to be armed with your own valuation and be confident with expert help that this is the way to calculate your business. The court will look at the most credible expert evidence on this, so get this done early.

Your estimate of any Capital Gains Tax that would be payable if you were to dispose of your business now

This question goes hand in hand with the valuation of the business in the previous questions. Importantly, you will need help from an accountant to make sure you approach the tax question credibly. It does not stop you from giving a worst-case scenario, but usually, tax mitigation needs to be included.

Net value of your interest in this business after any Capital Gains Tax liability

This is an arithmetic question taking away the tax liability from the value of the business. You will of course need to include your individual interest. So, if you had 4 partners/directors (and it is in accordance with the shareholders or partnership agreement), the interest might be one quarter.

> Tip:
> You could include costs of sale of the business such as agent's fee and legal costs.

Question 2.12 – List any directorships you hold or have held in the last 12 months (other than those already disclosed in Section 2.11)

You might have "earning" directorships (non-executive director) and this needs to be included here. This would be easy to check with Companies House.

Part 4 Capital: Pensions and Pension Protection Fund (PPF) Compensation

First some definitions:

PPF – Pension Protection Fund – a scheme to protect final salary or Defined benefits scheme (note; this does not protect money purchase schemes which is the vast majority of pensions).

CE – Cash Equivalent value, also known as CETV or Cash Equivalent Transfer Value.
   This is the most important figure used in financial proceedings. It is a useful way for courts to value pensions.
However, be aware that if you have a final salary scheme or a scheme provided by the Police service or civil service, the CE value may not be a good indicator of true value and an expert valuation may be needed.

Occupational pension schemes – Provided by employers on a generous scheme.

Final Salary or Defined Benefits – This used to be popular but has mostly been stopped by employers. It is the most valuable type of pension with generous benefits.

Money Purchase or Defined Contribution – Usual type of pension. Such schemes provide benefits on retirement based on the amount of money that has been paid into the scheme (by the employer and employee); how long the money has been invested and the level of charges (charges for running the scheme are usually a percentage) and the returns over this period (how much the investment has risen or fallen).

SIP – Self-invested pension.

NRA – Normal Retirement Age.

This will change in accordance with government regulations and will vary according to your age. If you are 50 years of age then your NRA is 67. The government website https://www.gov.uk/state-pension-age is a good place to check.

How do I approach this section on Pensions?

1. You could send this form to your pension provider to help you fill it in. This usually does not elicit any results but simply a letter enclosing the last statement.
2. Your pension company will have a helpline number. This is a good start to get the ball rolling in getting the information.
3. Look at your pension statement and find the information. Your pension provider must send you an annual statement.
4. If you have not received a statement, it is worth writing to them as they may have the wrong contact details for you. It is an obligation that they must provide a CE value statement within 3 months of the request.

What information do I need to include?
- The current value of your pension
- The contributions that have been paid into the scheme since starting the pension.
- How much pension and tax-free cash the plan is likely to pay out if you take your benefits at your retirement age (check your retirement age from the government site above).

- Details of any bonuses or rewards available under your plan, and if there are any conditions attached to receiving them.
- The transfer value of the plan (CE value)
- How you can transfer to another pension provider and what the charges are. This should be in your pension notes.
- The amount payable on death.
- Confirm if you have nominated anyone to receive your pension or any 'payments on death' benefits. Ask them to send you a form if you need to change this.
- Does the plan include contracted-out benefits and what were the dates you were contracted out?

What needs to be attached to your Form E for the pension section?
a. A recent statement showing the cash equivalent (CE). You would receive this each year from your pension provider for each pension.
b. If you do not have a valuation of your pension then you would need to give the estimated date when it will be available. You must attach a copy of your letter to the pension company showing that you have requested this information.

Is the pension in payment or drawdown?
You need to confirm here whether the pension is in payment or you are drawing down the pension.

State the CE quotation, the additional state pension valuation or PPF valuation of those rights
The Cash Equivalent value should be stated clearly on any statement that you receive. You will find this in any pension document received from the pension company when they update you yearly on your pension. If you do not have this, you can request this from the pension company free of charge.

If the arrangement is an occupational pension arrangement that is paying reduced CEs, please quote what the CE would have been if not reduced. If this is not possible, please indicate if the CE quoted is reduced CE

Sometimes, occupational pension schemes pay a reduced CE. This is stated in your statement. There should be two figures in your statement; one is for the reduced sum and the other is the figure without reduction. You need to include both. If, for some reason, you do not have the figures and your pension has been reduced, then all you need to do at this stage is to indicate it is, but raise this in the additional information.

Is the PPF compensation capped? (Please answer Yes or No)

The total amount of PPF compensation you can receive each year (payable if your pension is insufficient) is capped at a certain level, although most people who have a pension are not affected by this cap. From 1 April 2021, the cap at age 65 has been set at £41,461.

This will be made clear in your pension statement. If not, you should ask your pension provider.

Is my pension worth pound for pound, i.e., can you consider them as truly cash equivalent?

CE (Cash Equivalent) values are a good starting point for determining the valuation of pensions. However, you may be way off the actual value if the pension is small or very large; you are near to retirement; or, the condition of the policy is a final salary scheme. So, do not necessarily accept the face value when negotiating whether you wish to protect your pension or are seeking a pension order.

Should I ask my spouse for money or the pension?

This question should never be asked in isolation from the overall matrimonial pot.

Also, it depends on your age, how near you are to retirement and the likelihood of you having a solid period of continuous self/employment to get up to speed with pension contributions.

The rule of thumb is that large pensions may have large costs attached to them when it comes to splitting the pension. Sharing a pension may be more advisable. You should only decide this after speaking to your solicitor.

Why should I be suspicious of my spouse's true value of pension?

Be mindful that the CE can be misleading with regards to some pensions such as final salary schemes, those in the police/civil service, or those in payment which may be undervalued.

The CE values for a pension on divorce can be valued at significantly less than their true value. This could be due to the CE value being calculated for a person leaving their employment and taking their pension but on divorce, the spouse is still a member. Therefore, there needs to be an adjusted CE value to take this into account.

Take advice from a pension specialist; the cost of such advice can be worthwhile. It will also form part of your overall tax planning after divorce.

2 Financial Details Part 5 Capital: Other assets

2.14 Give details of any other assets not listed in Parts 1 to 4 above.

INCLUDE (the following list is not exhaustive):• Any personal or business assets not yet disclosed• Unrealisable assets• Share option schemes, stating the estimated net sale proceeds of the shares if the options were capable of exercise now, and whether Capital Gains Tax or income tax would be payable• Business expansion schemes• Futures• Commodities• Trust interests (including interests under a discretionary trust), stating your estimate of the value of the interest and when it is likely to become realisable. If you say it will never be realisable or has no value, give your reasons• Any asset that is likely to be received in the foreseeable future• Any asset held on your behalf by a third party• Any asset not disclosed elsewhere on this form even if held outside England and Wales.

You are reminded of your obligation to disclose all your financial assets and interests of ANY nature.

Here, you need to give details of other assets not listed previously.

- Any personal or business assets not yet disclosed

a. Unrealisable assets – Assets which cannot be sold for some reason. This can be because the time to realise them has not been triggered or certain conditions have not been met. This could be monies held in a trust such as a discretionary trust, an option or where the assets have not matured. It might also include Futures or commodities.
b. Share option schemes – This would be part of your employment like a Sharesave scheme. Such schemes may give you an example of the net proceeds if you were to exercise them now.
c. You should include a crypto-currency valuation.

You should consider the following:
- You need to check whether any capital gains tax is due on exercising them now.
- You need to give a value now and the value when it matures or when it can be realised. You must state when you anticipate the value to be realised.
- If, however, you think that the values cannot be realised at all, you will need to explain why.
- You must also include here any asset which is held by another on your behalf. You need to explain why it is being held, for how long and when it can be realised.
- Any asset that is likely to be received in the foreseeable future.
- Note: the assets above can be in the UK or abroad.

This section is important and if you are not sure whether to put in an asset or potential asset, speak to your lawyer.

How should I value the assets?
An internet value is sufficient at this stage, for example, for the value of shares or commodifies. Attach a print of the valuation page.

Total net value of the asset – What does this mean?
You may hold the asset in your name but you do not own it or have any beneficial interest.

There may be capital gains tax that you may need to pay, so state what this might be.

There might be costs of sale, e.g., professional fees.

2 Financial Details Part 6 Income: Earned income from employment

This part looks at your income in the last financial year. If it has changed or is about to change, then you need to explain this on a separate page.
You must have the following ready to attach to Form E:

1. P60 for the last financial year (you should have received this from your employer shortly after the last 5th of April)
2. Your last three payslips
3. Your last Form P11D if you have been issued with one

Job title and brief details of the type of work you do

I am about to change jobs – Write about the current job and the new job on separate sheets, making it clear that this is the job you are about to start. If you are unemployed and about to start a job then insert the details of the new job.

I am about to lose my job – You still need to complete this section and then explain when it will come to an end.

I do periodic or ad hoc work – You need to state the type of jobs you do and rely on the work you have done so far and what you did last year.

I am self-employed – Do not complete this section. You need to go to the next section Part 7.

Hours worked per week in this employment

What if my hours are different every week? – You need to explain this and give an average number of hours.

What if I am on a zero-hours contract? – Again, give an average amount of hours a week, say, over the last 3 to 6 months you have done.

Do I need to include overtime? – You need to give your basic hours, and, if you regularly do overtime, you need to state this and an average amount of overtime per week.

How long have you been with this employer?

What if I am contracting or freelancing? – You need to make clear your daily rate and average income for the year before. Explain if the contract is about to come to an end. Make clear any void periods of employment in the last few years to show that a void period is possible.

Explain the basis of your income i.e. state whether it is based on an annual salary or an hourly rate of pay and whether it includes commissions or bonuses

You need to set this out clearly.

We suggest you approach this in the following way:
- State your P60
- Basic Salary (look at your current contract or payslip)
- Commission
- Bonus

Briefly explain any other entries on the attached payslips other than basic income, income tax and national insurance

Some terms which you may not be sure about and which can appear on payslips:

Deductions: *These may be for loans or extra pension contributions* to
- **Total gross pay:** *This is the sum you receive under the contract on a monthly basis*
- **Gross for tax:** *This is the total of your income that will be subject to income tax*

- **Earnings for NI:** *This is the total of your income that will be subject to National Insurance*
- **Tax paid TD** – *Tax paid to date, this is a rolling total of tax paid*
- **Payment Period** – *This is the payment the payslip covers*
- **Earnings for NI TD** – *Earnings for National Insurance to date; this is a rolling total of the income on which National Insurance is calculated*
- **Pension contributions** – *What pension contributions you and your employer have made*
- **National Insurance TD** – *Rolling total of National Insurance paid*

My last three months are not an accurate reflection of my normal income; what should I do?

This could be because:

1. More or less overtime undertaken
2. Bonus or commission which is either more or less than usual
3. Your job has come to an end

You need to explain this, otherwise, the court will consider this income in calculating maintenance and capital.

Details and value of any bonuses or other occasional payments that you receive from this employment not otherwise already shown, including the basis upon which they are paid

Occasional payments could include:

1. Bonuses
2. Commission
3. Tips

You should include your contract showing that such payments are contractual or an email from your employer confirming why you have been paid and on what basis this payment has been made. It is important always to emphasise that these are non-contractual and discretionary. It is important to note that courts are looking for regular payments and although they may be discretionary, the court could assume that you will continue to receive such payments.

> **Tip:**
> It is important to show clearly that these payments are not regular and may be discretionary, otherwise, the court could conclude that these payments should be treated as being received regularly and include them in any income consideration.

If my spouse receives a bonus but that bonus may be variable, how can I determine the level of maintenance that should be paid?
The approach is to calculate a total figure for the vital maintenance to cover the ordinary expenses of the other spouse together with any additional discretionary items; to make a monthly order to be paid from the salary at whatever rate the Judge feels to be fair, and for the balance to be expressed as a percentage of the net bonus up to a stated maximum each year. In the case of H –v- W (2013 appeal), the Judge imposed a cap of £20,000 per annum on the wife's share of 25% of the husband's future bonus on the discretionary items.

Details and value of any benefits in kind, perks or other remuneration received from this employer in the last year (e.g. provision of a car, payment of travel, accommodation, meal expenses, etc.)
You will need to produce your contract of employment or a side letter giving details of such benefits.

You will also need to include Sharesave schemes or stock options.

Your estimate of your net income from this employment for the next 12 months. If this differs significantly from your current income, explain why in box 4.1.2
This is an important question for the court to look at. This information will be used by the court to determine maintenance and even capital division.

If your income is anticipated to change, then you need to explain this here.

You should include any correspondence with your employer showing changes to your income. This could include:

1. Consultation letter for redundancy
2. Letter of termination
3. Letter showing a change of salary or new contract of employment
4. Notice of reduction of overtime
5. Fixed-term contract

If none of these are available, give as much information as possible. Courts will regard any changes in income, particularly a reduction of income, only if there is cogent evidence.

What courts **do not** consider as factors to show reduced income:

1. Overtime drying up.
2. Possible redundancy – unless you are on a formal consultation period.
3. Fixed-term contracts not being renewed if, for the previous years, the contract has been extended.
4. A period of furlough in work, if there was no previous void period.
5. A downturn in the economy.

I am deciding to stop my overtime; how does this affect the financial division?
You should take care that if you stop overtime for reasons related to the divorce, for example, if the overtime has been historically consistent but then it stops before or during the divorce, then the courts may simply ignore that you have given up your overtime.

Your income historically or your true realisable income is called Potential Earning Capacity. It is expected that you are working at your full potential. If your employer has stopped overtime, then this will have an impact on maintenance. As long as the cut in overtime is not your fault, then it will not adversely affect you.

Part 7 Income: Income from self-employment or partnership

2.16 – You will have already given details of your business and provided the last two years' accounts in section 2.11. Complete this section giving details of your income from your business. Complete one page for each business.

What documents do you need to include in Form E for this section?
Two years' accounts – this is the last two complete years.
Documentation required for attachment to this section:

a. A copy of your last tax assessment or, if that is not available, a letter from your accountant confirming your tax liability.
b. If net income from the last financial year and estimated net income for the next 12 months are significantly different, a copy of management accounts for the period since your last account or draft accounts for the coming year if these are available.

Do you have to provide the current year's accounts?
Only if your accountant has prepared this. They may be unaudited accounts.

This section is to be completed with the benefit of the accounts already prepared by your accountant.

You must complete this for each business.

If you have no accounts or you have just started, then an estimate or management account would be a useful guide.

> **Tip:**
> You should be aware that any new business may be asked for a business plan or projections given by you to your bank to get a loan or on any promotional material showing the potential of any business if it is a franchise business or business that you have purchased.

Name of the business
This is as it appears on the Companies House register.
You should also put in your trading name.
If you are a sole trader then state the name as registered with HMRC.

Date on which your last accounts were completed
This refers to audited accounts or completed accounts as submitted to HMRC or lodged at Companies House.

Your share of gross business profit from the last completed accounts
This will depend on how many people are in your business and your arrangement for profit share. This could be by way of a shareholders' agreement (which will need to be produced) or another such agreement. If you do not have an agreement in writing, explain separately how the profits have been divided between your business partners. The accountant should already have indicated in the accounts how the profits will be shared/distributed. An accountant's letter would be useful here.

Income tax and national insurance payable on your share of gross business profit above
The above question relates to gross profits (before tax) and the court needs to know how much tax you will pay on your share of gross profits. This can be found in your business tax return or your personal tax return. Don't forget that you may be paying voluntary national insurance contributions and these need to be included here.
You may need a letter from your accountant if these figures are not readily apparent.

Net income for that year (using the two figures directly above, gross business profits less income tax and national insurance payable)
This can be a purely arithmetical figure based on taking away your tax in the last answer and the gross profits. But again, a letter from an accountant will provide good evidence if the accounts or tax returns do not do so.

Details and value of any benefits in kind (P11D), perks or other remuneration received from this business in the last year e.g. provision of a car, payment of travel, accommodation, meal expenses, etc.

This is an important question and your spouse will be aware of any benefits you take from the business, so best to make frank disclosure to avoid expensive legal costs in pursuing this line of questioning. The usual culprits are cars and travel when personal expenses can be disguised as business expenses.

Amount of any regular monthly or other drawings that you take from this business

Sometimes the self-employed will take a basic salary, and this can be included here or it could be included in the employed part but either way, it needs to be made clear that this is a salary rather than drawings. Drawings can be easily shown on your bank statement. If the drawings are irregular, maybe because they are only taken when there is enough cash in the business, then an accountant's letter would help to show average drawings from the business over the year.

If the estimated figure directly below is different from the net income as at the end date of the last completed accounts, briefly explain the reason(s)

This question is about whether your profits from the last accounting period accurately reflect the true position for the next accounting period

This answer needs to be carefully teased out and most miss the opportunity to explain in sufficient detail the reason for the estimated income being different from previous years. The usual answers found here are "downturn in business", "challenging economic conditions" "Covid" or "Brexit". Courts take very little notice of such platitudes unless there are some meaningful details.

You may wish to include any articles from the trade journal or national newspaper showing how your industry is expected to do in the coming year and the challenges faced by your trade or service.

Include an accountant's letter giving details of why there may be a change in the fortune of the company.

Provide an application for an overdraft facility to indicate that you may need to resort to short-term funding.

Also, give a short narrative on the challenges faced by the company, for example, loss of orders or business clients, increased competition, loss of key personnel or government policy.

Your estimate of your net annual income for the next 12 months
This is an estimate and you will be able to state whether your income will go up, down or stay the same. The court will have effectively 3 years' accounts – two years' previous accounts as required to be included with Form E and the current account period. This may have been produced by the time the case comes to court or else your spouse will seek management accounts to show the state of accounts for the current year, but, in any event, this will give the court a sufficient period to be able to show a trend of your income.

Estimated TOTAL of ALL net income from self-employment or partnership for the next 12 months: TOTAL I
This is the total of all the income from all the businesses you have an interest in. So, this should be the total "Net annual income for the last 12 months" for each business and you should have completed this page for each business.

Part 8 Income: Income from investments e.g. dividends, interest or rental income

Question 2.17 – Details of income received in the last financial year (the year ended last 5th April), and your estimate of your income for the current financial year. Indicate whether the income was paid gross or net of income tax. You are not required to calculate any tax payable that may arise.

You should direct yourself to your tax return which will summarise all your various income from all sources. If there are new sources of income not included in the tax return for the previous year then you should include them here.

Nature of income and the asset from which it is derived

Names of shares or investments, rental, loan interest or dividends should state clearly the source of the income.

You need not state individual shares but class them as shares unless you have one or two.

On rental income, you may need to divide them up in accordance with the respective properties.

Paid gross or net – whether the income is paid before or after deductions.

Income received in the last financial year.

Estimated income for the next year.

Part 9 Income: Income from state benefits (including state pension and child benefit)

Question 2.18 – Details of all state benefits that you are currently receiving.

Benefits can include:

1. Tax Credits
2. Child Benefit
3. State pension
4. Child care vouchers
5. Any other state benefits.

You need to include the estimate of these benefits for the coming 12 months. If they may be different, then explain why on a separate sheet.

Part 10 Income: Any other income

Question 2.19 – Details of any other income not disclosed above.

This is a mop-up question. If you are unsure where to include any type of income that is not covered elsewhere, this is where you should include it.

You should include:
- Cash-in-hand income
- Ad hoc work
- Income earned by your children

This is where you should include any private or occupational pensions that you received

Also, there may be income which you are likely to receive during the next 12 months, so you should include the following information:

Nature of income
Give as much detail as you can about where this income is coming from.

Paid gross or net
Is this income paid before tax has been deducted or after tax has been deducted?

Income received in the last financial year
This is the total income received (but which you have not accounted for elsewhere) for the last financial year.

Estimated income for the next 12 months.
If your income is going to change from the previous year, you need to explain this on a separate sheet.

Summaries

Question 2.20 – Summary of your capital (Parts 1 to 5).

You should now take each figure from each of the lettered sections and insert the details in the summary box.

> Current value of your interest in the family home A
> Current value of your interest in all other property B
> Current value of your interest in personal assets C
> Current value of your interest in business assets E
> Current value of your pension and PPF compensation assets F
> Current value of all your other assets G

Once you have totalled this, you need to take away your liabilities which are listed in section D and the net total of your assets will be inserted in the final box.

Question 2.21 – Summary of your estimated income for the next 12 months (Parts 6 to 10)

It is important to appreciate that courts are interested in total estimated income for the coming 12 months, so getting these right and justifying the sum will put you in a good position to mount a more persuasive case, particularly as this will impact maintenance (what you may have to pay to your spouse or receive from your spouse) and capital provision.

You should now take each figure from each of the lettered sections and insert the details in the summary box.

> Estimated net total of income from employment H
> Estimated net total of income from self-employment or partnership I
> Estimated net total of investment income J
> Estimated state benefit receipts K
> Estimated net total of all other income L

Then total all the estimated income for the next 12 months by adding H to L

3 Financial Requirements Part 1 Income needs

Question 3.1 Income needs for yourself and for any children living with you or provided for by you.

*ALL figures should be annual, monthly or weekly (state which). You **must not** use a combination of these periods. State your current income needs and, if these are likely to change in the near future, explain the anticipated change and give an estimate of the future cost.*

*This section will determine **maintenance provision and also capitalised** needs. This means that if your needs outstrip your income, it could mean a larger capital settlement.*

Why is this section important?
This section must include income needs for yourself and for any children living with you or those children you are supporting.

How are you going to state the figures – Annually, Monthly or Weekly?
You must decide how you wish to approach this. Are you intending to state all the figures annually, monthly or weekly? You need to state this clearly. ALL figures should be annual, monthly or weekly (state which). It is recommended that you use monthly as

What do I put in this section and why is this important?
I anticipate my income needs are going to change because:
   Here, you need to include the following:
   What are your **current** income needs? So, how much do you actually need to live on now? This needs to be a figure (which you will justify in the next section). You now need to write down how these may change in the future and what the changes will be. Again, you need to state a figure (which you justify later).
   You now need to explain the reasons for the change.

This could be because you will be living in separate households or you might be moving out.

Your spouse may be moving out.

Children may be moving out or leaving for university.

Question 3.1.1 Income needs for yourself

This is just for yourself.

Expenses like food and housing costs and utilities can be combined and do not need to be split. The rule of thumb here is where the costs are wholly and exclusively for the children, this can be included in the next section.

Question 3.1.2 Income needs for your children

Now include any **additional** needs for the children.

You can include, lunches, tuition, school trips, uniform, clothes, haircuts and anything needed for school.

This is an important part of the document and needs to be carefully completed when completing Form E. However, Form E does not provide for a comprehensive categorisation of the different expenses.

An **example of a Schedule of Expenses and Outgoings** can be found in **Appendix 2**. You should attach this to your Form E and simply state in this section 'see attached' (and state where it can be found). Read the section on how to arrange Form E.

This schedule will help in determining the following issues:

- What you need to live on.
- Maintenance you may need or should receive.
- What maintenance you can afford to pay (your outgoings will be a marker of affordability in calculating spousal maintenance (also known as periodic payments; this is a payment which is paid to you on top of any child maintenance).
- Whether you can afford to live at your current property.
- Whether you need to consider making changes to your lifestyle on separation or divorce.

- Which expenses the court will take into account and not take into account when assessing needs.
- Whether you need a larger capital sum from the matrimonial pot.

How should I approach completing the Expense Schedule?

First rule – Don't guess the figures. You will be questioned on them by your spouse's solicitors and even asked to justify them with any supporting documents at Court (by way of cross-examination at any final trial).

Before you start on this form:

Take out your bank and credit card statements. Work out in broad categories what you spend on a monthly basis e.g. food, toiletries, children's activities, eating out, etc.

These documents will help to show your spouse where you got these figures from. Remember, you need to produce to the Court and your spouse at least 12 months' bank statements (not credit card statements although these could be asked for if you show a large credit card debt).

Do not exaggerate your needs. This is because your spouse's solicitors will be conducting a forensic examination of how you have come to the figures and ask you questions about it. If you then later have to amend your figures, this places obvious scrutiny on the rest of your Form E.

Use the Schedule in Appendix 2

The Schedule is split into two parts – Current and Future figures. This is an important distinction. Future expenses should represent those expenses you might have after divorce or separation. So, the current schedule will have to tally with your bank and credit card statements and those you have increased or decreased will have to be explained.

When considering future expenses, you need to adjust your figures as follows:

- Take into account the single-person discount in Council Tax. Go to your local authority website to work this out.

- If you are not sure of the cost of holidays or upkeep of the house, use average figures over three years (do not include large expenses like repairs, as these come under Capital needs). Holiday expenses should be average holiday costs taken during marriage (taking into consideration one less person).
- Food and toiletries may be less.
- Nursery/child-minding costs may be more.
- Rental Costs if you are moving out and associated costs of renting (moving, storage, extra travelling).
- Don't forget to include AVC (additional voluntary contributions from your wages), Work Savings Schemes, etc.; – although they are taken from your wages, they should still be considered as outgoings.
- Travel costs to see the children

Do not include:

- Capital expenses such as boiler repair; this goes in the Capital Needs part of Form E.
- Rent paid to parents when previously, no such arrangement existed. However, board and contribution towards expenses of your parents' home are reasonable.
- Grandparents charging for looking after your children.
- Payments for loans to family and friends when none existed previously.

If your costs suddenly change then you have an ongoing obligation to keep both your spouse and the Court advised. Certainly, before any hearing, you need to review this schedule.

Can I include Sky TV and Gym membership?
This is a reasonable expense to include.

What is not a reasonable expense?

- Those you anticipate but have not yet expended (this should be included in a different section in Form E).

- Expenses for an "aspirational lifestyle". The expenses should be similar to those you had whilst you were married.
- You cannot include gambling or other vices as a reasonable expense.
- Giving money to family unless they are reliant on it.

How much do I put down for food, toiletries, etc?
Look at your bank/credit card statement for 12 months and work out an average. Do not exaggerate these expenses as they can easily be worked out from your bank statements and credit card statements.

Can I claim savings and pension provision?
If you are a regular saver or have been putting money in a savings account then you can.

3 Financial Requirements Part 2 Capital needs

Question 3.2 Set out below the reasonable future capital needs for yourself and for any children living with you or provided for by you.

This question deals with what capital you need. This means your future needs which are not related to income such as house, car, special equipment for a disability, etc. This is a consolidation of needs for you and your children.

Question 3.2.1 Capital needs for yourself.
INCLUDE: All capital needs for yourself; capital needs for any children living with you or provided for by you but only if these form part of your total capital needs (e.g. housing, car, etc.)

What should I put for my housing needs?
You should approach this in the following way:
   You should consider your housing needs for yourself and your children. Number of rooms needed, where you wish to live and why; e.g., near their school.

Question 3.2.2 Capital needs for children living with you or provided for by you.

Do not repeat any capital needs that you have already dealt with for yourself like housing and car. These must be particular capital needs, and these may include: Special equipment for a disability

Any needs to assist with the children's learning/schooling

How to cost out the capital needs.

Housing: To approach the housing issue, this needs to be carefully considered in consultation with your solicitor.

The primary question that courts focus on is reasonable housing needs. Most tend towards a "wish list". If you exaggerate a housing need, you may discredit your case, particularly if it is not in line with the party's standard of living.

Spouses consider that an inflated housing need will bolster their case on capital, but all it does is helps the other spouse to justify their own inflated housing needs. It also means more legal fees and court time needs to be expended to deal with establishing reasonable housing need.

How do I approach housing need?

Look at:

How many bedrooms you need

Which area you are looking in and why

Any special requirements for the house, e.g., no stairs, close to station

Then go to Rightmove or Zoopla and find appropriate properties. You will need this evidence at a later stage.

Car

These are the considerations:

How many seats?

What car do you have now?

Second-hand/new/lease?

Special equipment – State each type of item and a price range.

4 Other Information

4.1 Details of any significant changes in your assets or income.
In both sections 4.1.1 and 4.1.2,

INCLUDE:
- ALL assets held both within and outside England and Wales
- The disposal of any asset

Question 4.1.1 Significant changes in assets or income during the LAST 12 months.

This question is dealing with asset acquisition and disposal – those assets you have purchased and sold in the last 12 months. It must include all assets in the UK and abroad.

This section includes buying and selling assets such as property, shares, and chattels (like cars and antiques). It also includes assets that have been gifted to you or you have inherited.

This question deals with income changes in the last 12 months. This would include:

1. Increase or reduction in overtime – explain here if this is temporary.
2. Secured or lost employment in the last 12 months.
3. If self-employed income has changed – explain the circumstances here.

4.1.2 Significant changes in assets or income likely to occur during the NEXT 12 months

This is usually left blank and is a missed opportunity to show decreases in wealth (or increases).

Assets

This question is dealing with your intention to acquire or your expectation to receive assets in the **coming** 12 months.

What if I am not sure when I will be purchasing or receiving property in the coming 12 months?

The word is "likely". The following factors may help you decide whether it will be likely, and, more importantly, what courts would expect you to include:

1. If there has been a death and you are a beneficiary of the will or by way of intestacy, even if it is early days and probate has not yet been granted.
2. You have put an offer in for a property but you have not exchanged or completed.
3. There is an agreement to pay you an amount or transfer an asset within 12 months.
4. If there is the possibility of you receiving or acquiring an asset in over 12 months, then this does not have to be included.

Income

This question deals with income changes in the next 12 months. This would include:

1. If you have been given a promotion or a review of your salary. The courts would look at previous increases in wages, and, if there has been a consistent increase, then there would be an expectant increase in the coming 12 months. If this is not going to be the case, it is best to substantiate this with evidence such as appraisal scores or correspondence with your employer.
2. Expected bonus. Again, the court appreciates that bonuses are not guaranteed but if you have received bonuses consistently in previous years, then the courts would expect to take account of such a bonus in future years. This would also include commission. It is important for you to show any evidence if this is not the case.

   Such evidence would include:

   a. Projections of commission
   b. Correspondence from employer
   c. Appraisals
   d. Company announcements

3. If you are under consultation for redundancy, you will need to show a letter from your employer. You will also have to estimate what redundancy package you may receive. It is important to note that courts do not take account general threats of redundancy or downturn in the economy.
4. Reduction in overtime. Although overtime is voluntary, courts expect you to maintain the levels of overtime previously worked. If there truly is an overtime ban or reduction, a letter would need to be produced by the employer.
5. Seasonal work or temporary assignments. Again, courts expect you to maintain previous levels of employment. You would need a letter from your recruitment consultant to show there has been a genuine downturn in such work.

Question 4.2 Brief details of the standard of living enjoyed by you and your spouse/civil partner during the marriage/civil partnership.

Why is this question being asked and what is the court trying to ascertain here?

1. The courts are assessing lifestyles to enable them to assess the fundamental question of the needs of the parties.
2. If you say you have two holidays a year, and, in the schedule of expenses, the family have consistently had two holidays, then it would be difficult to object to such expenses. However, the courts do expect a certain restraint in dealing with such luxuries.
3. If you are the receiving party of maintenance, this is a helpful section to complete as fully as possible as this will assist with working out your spousal maintenance claim (uplift on the children's maintenance).
4. What to include: holidays (where and type of holidays and how frequent), holiday home, private school for children, types of cars driven, membership of clubs or associations, hobbies, social life such as how many times you eat out and gym membership.

Question 4.3 Are there any particular contributions to the family property and assets or outgoings, or to family life, or the welfare of the family that have been made by you, your partner or anyone else that you think should be taken into account?

If there are any such items, briefly describe the contribution and state the amount, when it was made and by whom.

INCLUDE: Contributions already made. Contributions that will be made in the foreseeable future.

This question is seeking to find out whether you have made contributions whether financial or otherwise to the marriage.

If you had to give up your career to look after the children, this is your chance to show it here. You would need to show:

Details of your income (and pension) before you had children

Any prospects of promotion and career path (an up-to-date CV would be useful)

Note

You should take note that this could help your spouse to make the case against you, that your evidence would point to your potential earning capacity, which you could achieve again, thereby dampening your claim for capital or income.

Can I mention here any money/assets that I brought into the marriage?

This is your chance to state all the assets (including money) brought into the marriage.

Were your assets kept together or separate during the marriage?

It is important to state clearly if any of the assets were used for the family or kept separate. It is a more compelling argument that assets which have been brought into the marriage have been kept separate.

This is to persuade the court that such assets should remain yours particularly (only if the remaining assets are more than sufficient to meet the needs of the parties). For example, if you had a buy-to-let property which you have kept distinct from the marriage (i.e. not mingled those assets or income with marital assets).

This can be particularly helpful in short marriages or where there is a pre-nuptial agreement. It is important to state details here by producing the agreement and, in particular, the financial schedules attached to it to show the level of contribution.

What if members of my family have contributed to the asset?
If other members of the family contributed to the family assets or income, such as parents, then you need to state clearly all the information for the court to see if this interest needs to be preserved.

> **Tip:**
> If there is a trust deed or if the assets are in your name but the true owner may be someone else, you must explain this.
>
> If the school fees have been paid by the parents of your spouse, then it is a good argument that such an arrangement is likely to continue. However, courts do not have the powers to order third parties to pay such expenses.

Question 4.3 Are there any particular contributions to the family property and assets or outgoings, or to family life, or the welfare of the family that have been made by you, your partner or anyone else that you think should be taken into account? If there are any such items, briefly describe the contribution and state the amount, when it was made and by whom.

INCLUDE:

- Contributions already made
- Foreseeable future

The following, which are seen in Form Es, are usually <u>not relevant:</u>

I have been the breadwinner of the family

I paid the mortgage

I paid for all the outgoings

I paid for everything and my spouse stayed at home looking after the children

I was the only one contributing; my spouse contributed nothing

This question is asking about the following circumstances:

1. What was brought into the marriage?
2. Was there a pre-nuptial agreement
3. If this is a short marriage, then what assets were brought into the marriage?
4. Did someone other than the parties pay for the deposit or refurbishment of the home?
5. Did a family member help with outgoings such as school fees?
6. Was there an interest-free loan given?

How can someone who has interest in the matrimonial asset make a claim?

This section is important if, for example, a parent has helped one of the parties to set up home and that person may need their interest noted. For instance, if, at the time the parties married, a loan or an amount was given to the couple to buy their first home and the money was not a gift, then the parents need to 'intervene' in the divorce proceedings. This means they need their interest in the home taken into account and given back to them in the division of the finances. Intervenor actions are always difficult to establish if there is no written documentation, such as a trust deed. The intervenor (usually the parents) will need to have separate legal representation and usually, their contribution is disputed. In such a situation, the case is divided into two. The intervenor action goes first to determine whether their interest should be ring-fenced and returned (and therefore the matrimonial pot reduced) and thereafter, the matrimonial pot is more easily identified before courts look at how to fairly divide the finances.

Question 4.4 – Bad behaviour or conduct by the other party will only be taken into account in very exceptional circumstances when deciding how assets should be shared after divorce/dissolution. If you feel it should be taken into account in your case, identify the nature of the behaviour or conduct below.

This is an important section, but, more often than not, this is filled out incorrectly which leads the courts to ignore what is said here.

What is <u>not</u> bad behaviour?

1. Repeating what is in the divorce petition
2. Dealing with the behaviour which you regard as the bad behaviour of your former spouse
3. What is annoying about your former spouse
4. What you hate about what he/she has done to you

What can be included here?
Actions by your former spouse that have meant that you have suffered a direct financial detriment. For example:

<u>Domestic Violence</u>

If there has been domestic violence which has meant you could not work or that you have had to take time off work, or that this has curtailed your ability to find a job.

<u>Financial recklessness</u>

If your spouse has been reckless in financial decisions or has lost money as a result of negligence in looking after the family finances. This does not include bad luck or just losing money in a business or due to economic or other factors outside their control. If such recklessness can be proved or established, then the court could adjust any award to reflect such losses.

Vice

If your spouse is a gambler or has lost money as a result of a vice such as alcohol or spending money on something that is not for the benefit of the family.

Giving away money

This could be to family or friends. This does not include reasonable gifts or donations to charity.

Creating debts

This could be debt on a credit card or by purchasing an expensive car that the family could ill afford. If, however, the expenses are directly or indirectly used for the family, then this might be treated as reasonable even if the expenditure is unreasonable.

Question 4.4 – Give details of any other circumstances that you consider could significantly affect the extent of the financial provision to be made by or for you or any child of the family. INCLUDE (the following list is not exhaustive):

- Earning capacity
- Disability
- Inheritance prospects
- Redundancy
- Retirement
- Any agreement made between you and your spouse/civil partner before or after your marriage/civil partnership stating whether or not you rely upon the agreement giving your reasons
- Any plans to marry, form a civil partnership or live with a new partner
- Any contingent liabilities

This is probably the most important section in Form E. It is a squandered opportunity if this section is not completed properly.

What is this section about?

1. It allows you to put in all the information in narrative form to explain the figures in Form E.
2. It allows you to give clarification of the current figures and the anticipated figures

How do I present the information?

1. If you are explaining a section in Form E then head it up with the paragraph number; e.g.:
   2 Financial Details Part 5 Capital: Other assets
   2.14 Any asset held on your behalf by a third party
2. Use separate sheets of paper but make sure you write clearly.
   RIDER [means a supplementary sheet] TO PARAGRAPH 4.5 [referring to the question number] – PAGE [this is a number of additional pages]
3. When you are explaining the circumstances, do not forget to include any evidence.
4. The explanation does not need to be long but there needs to be enough information to indicate to the court that this is an issue which requires further investigation.

Question 4.6 If you have subsequently married or formed a civil partnership (or intend to) or are living with another person (or intend to), give brief details, so far as they are known to you, of his or her income, assets and liabilities.

This question covers the following situations:

- If you are married
- If you are engaged
- If you are living with a person and are in a relationship
- If you intend to live with someone in a relationship

Why are the courts asking this?

Courts take this into consideration for the following reasons:

1. Your overall expenditure will be reduced if you live with someone.
2. Your ability to borrow money will increase as you can use the other person's income to be factored into any mortgage calculation.
3. Your "effective" needs might be reduced as you are now in a relationship and may be able to depend on their income and assets.

I know only a limited amount of information about the other person – what should I say?

This is a difficult question to answer as you would need to know something about the other person's income and assets.

You can simply state general information, for example, if they own a property [include the address] but you may not know the amount of mortgage that is outstanding. You may know what they do but not know their salary.

The courts <u>cannot</u> force the other person to disclose such information. There is no obligation on the other person to cooperate with any questions or indeed produce any financial information.

You can provide any limited information you have on the other person.

You may wish to provide more information; for example, the other person may have obligations such as paying maintenance to their own former spouse; they may be unwell or have a disability and you may need to care for them. This can help to mitigate their ability to reduce your overall needs.

What if the court has limited information about the income and assets of the other person?

The courts will infer from the information about the person's income and assets based on even the limited information you have given.

How will this information be used by the courts?

Any financial information concerning the other person will assist the court in establishing needs, whether maintenance or capital, such as housing.

5 Order Sought

5.1 If you are able at this stage, specify what kind of orders you are asking the court to make.

Even if you cannot be specific at this stage, if you are able to do so, indicate:
a) If the family home is still owned, whether you are asking for it to be transferred to yourself or your spouse/civil partner or whether you are saying it should be sold

This is a difficult question to answer at such an early stage of the court proceedings.

However, the court wants an idea of what you might like to happen. Any answer will not mean you are held to it nor will this actually affect the way the court will eventually decide the issue.

This question gives an indication to the court as to what the issues will be.

You can answer it in a number of ways. Note – this question relates to the capital or assets of the marriage, notably, the family home or other properties.

1. You may wish to simply state that the family home is to be sold and proceeds divided fairly and for the parties to then purchase their respective homes.
2. You could indicate that the property should not be sold so that you and the children can live there until the children are grown up.
3. You may ask the court to determine reasonable maintenance.
4. You can also put it here if you want the court to determine any interest of any third party, such as parents who have loaned you money.

b) Whether you consider this is a case for continuing spousal maintenance/maintenance for your civil partner or whether you see the case as being appropriate for a 'clean break' (A 'clean break' means a settlement or order which provides amongst other things, that neither you nor your spouse/civil partner will have any further claim against the income or capital of the other party. A 'clean break' does not terminate the responsibility of a parent to a child.)

This question relates to maintenance. Again, you can simply state "Appropriate for a clean break" which means that there should not be any order of maintenance, but instead, there should be an adjustment in the capital to make up for any income disparity. This means instead of giving maintenance, you are asking the court to give more capital to the other spouse to make up for the different levels of income.

It is important to read the second part of this question. A clean break does not mean an end to any type of maintenance obligation as the obligation of child maintenance is still preserved. However, your solicitor can advise you on how to mitigate such an obligation.

You may say this is "appropriate for maintenance". You do not need to state how much at this stage.

c) Whether you are seeking a
    i.   **Pension Sharing Order**
    ii. **Pension Attachment Order**
    iii. **Pension Compensation Sharing Order**
    iv. **Pension Compensation Attachment Order**

At this stage, it might be difficult to decide which one is more appropriate.

Why is the court asking this?
The court has to make some decisions early on in the case to decide whether to obtain an expert report on the pension to establish the precise value. Please note that the CETV is general guidance on pension values and some pensions, such as for the civil service or police, are more complicated and the CETV may not correctly reflect the true value. Also, one may be more appropriate depending on age, health and size of pension pot.

What do these mean?

<u>Pension Sharing Order</u>

This is a straightforward split of the pension; note that there may be rules on how to split the pension and how much it costs.

Pension Attachment Order
===

To make payment to the spouse of a proportion of the pension when the pension is drawn down i.e. in payment.

Pension Compensation Sharing Order
===

This is a court order requiring the pension to be split.

Pension Compensation Attachment Order
===

This is a court order requiring the pension to be paid when the pension is drawn down (i.e. in payment).

If you are not sure, then simply say "To be decided".

If you are seeking a transfer or settlement of any property or assets, identify the property or assets in question

This is a very important question and you need to list all the properties. This includes:

- Properties which are in joint names
- Property in your name only
- Property in which you have an interest but are not named on the title deeds.

I am to receive an inheritance as I am named as a beneficiary in a will – Do I need to include this here?

You do not need to include properties that you may have an interest in if, for example, a parent passes away. The reason for this is that a will could be changed – your interest is not guaranteed.

Question 5.2 If you are seeking a variation of an ante-nuptial or post-nuptial settlement or a relevant settlement made during, or in anticipation of, a civil partnership, identify the settlement, by whom it was made, its trustees and beneficiaries and state why you allege it is a settlement which the court can vary.

This question is appropriate if you are applying to vary a pre-nuptial or post-nuptial agreement.

Question 5.3 If you are seeking an avoidance of disposition order, or if you have already applied for such an order, identify the property to which the disposition relates and the person or body in whose favour the disposition is alleged to have been made.

This question relates to an application or future application, regarding a property or asset, which you are applying to stop the other spouse from disposing of or selling said property or asset.

You should immediately seek help from a solicitor to obtain an "S37 order". This is similar to a freezing injunction, freezing any such transaction. However, this must be done quickly, otherwise, it may be difficult to trace or recover assets.

<u>**Statement of Truth**</u>*delete as appropriate*

<u>*[I believe] [the Applicant/Respondent believes] that the facts stated in this statement are true</u>

<u>*I am duly authorised by the Applicant/Respondent to sign this statement</u>

<u>and confirm that the information given above is a full, frank, clear and accurate disclosure of my financial and other relevant circumstances.</u>

If you are signing this without lawyers, then delete *[the Applicant/Respondent believes]*

Then sign and date the form.

If you have submitted Form A, then you are the applicant so delete everything but the Applicant. If you received the financial remedy proceedings (regardless of whether you are the petitioner in the divorce) you are the Respondent.

Why do I have to sign a statement of truth on Form E?

This is because if there is inaccurate information or information that is missing, problems could arise later on with the following possible consequences:

Proceedings for contempt of court could be brought against a person who makes, or causes to be made, a false statement in a document verified by a statement of truth without an honest belief in its truth. You could be fined or sent to prison.

What if the missing or inaccurate information is discovered after the proceedings have finished?

Any agreement that you enter into or order can be set aside (i.e. it can be cancelled) if later it is found that the financial information is incorrect or incomplete.

Most likely to happen:
- A costs order can be made against you.
- Proceedings are delayed and more costs have to be paid by both parties.
- Your case may be discredited if this matter comes before the court.

If I have missed out something or have forgotten to put something in Form E, can I amend it?

Yes, you should do this immediately and explain why it was missed. It is important to be as frank as possible, otherwise, your case could be damaged.

Once Form E has been completed, do I need to keep collecting and keeping financial information?

Yes, as you will be asked to update your Form E before every hearing. You should also tell your solicitor if your financial circumstances change. You have an ongoing obligation to let the court and your spouse know if there is a change in your financial position.

Schedule of Documents to accompany Form E

The list on Form E shows the documents you must attach to your Form E if applicable. You may attach other documents where it is necessary to explain or clarify any of the information that you give in Form E.

What If I do not have the documents?
State clearly when you expect them to be produced and if necessary, give details of when you requested them and any correspondence showing that such a request has been made.

Where do I list the documents which are not mentioned in this list?
There is a section at the very end of the document. Though there is only space for one document, you can continue on a separate sheet. You can list (and attach) further documents by using the following tabular style.

Description of Document   Form E Reference   Attached/to follow

What if I have documents which I cannot get hold of because the account is now dormant or the bank does not produce statements?
If you have a dormant account, show the last statement and then explain the position in a short explanatory note.

What if I do not receive paper statements?
You should print them out from the internet or even take a screenshot of your internet bank statement.

Can my spouse be ordered to meet my legal costs if they delay or do not produce their financial information correctly?
It is not usual for courts to make costs orders and each party is expected to pay their own costs unless it is shown that one party has been unreasonable in the way they have conducted themselves, which could include delays in providing financial information or misleading the court.

Do I need to include my children's money in Form E?
Definitely, yes. This is counted as an asset of the marriage. This would include money given by grandparents. It would not include any assets held on a properly constituted trust where you, the parents, had no control. However, you must still reveal any money held in a trust.

Final points

Who do I need to send this to?
You need to send Form E and all the supporting documents to your spouse's solicitors and the court. The court address is on Form A.

The address on the divorce petition is different to the court for the financial proceedings; which court is it?
Sometimes the divorce is started in one court and then moved to a local or another court. Check Form A and any further order in relation to the financial proceedings to ascertain which is the allocated court for the financial remedy proceedings.

Should I send this by recorded delivery?
You should either send this by email or recorded delivery but not both.

Which email should I use?
There are many emails but there should be an email at the bottom of any order or Form A.
    If in doubt, use the general email when you search the court.

Should there be a covering letter when attaching Form E?
You should ensure there is a covering letter as below:
    Draft letter to the court

Dear Sir

Re: [insert case name e.g. John James Smith v Jane Sarah Smith]
[case number]
Date of any hearing

I refer to the order [state the date of the order and where you were ordered to file Form E]

Please find attached the Form and supporting documents to be filed. I confirm I have sent this to my wife's/husband's solicitors by [email or post]/ I have sent this to the court by email [when writing to the spouse].

Kindly acknowledge safe receipt.

Yours faithfully,

How should I serve Form E on my spouse?
This sounds like an odd question, but remember you are required to exchange Form Es. The other side may not be ready and you need to contact them to see if they are ready to exchange and agree on how this will be done.

Usually, it is agreed that the documents are posted on a certain day or else sent by email on a certain day and at a certain time.

What should the covering letter say to the other side?
Draft letter to the court

Dear Sir

Re: [insert case name e.g. John James Smith v Jane Sarah Smith]
[case number]
Date of any hearing

I refer to the order [state the date of the order where you were ordered to file Form E] and our agreement to exchange Form E by post/email.

Please find attached the Form and supporting documents to be filed. I have sent this to the court by email [when writing to the spouse]

Kindly acknowledge safe receipt.

Yours faithfully,

Should I delay in sending it to the court if the other side is not ready to exchange?
No, under no circumstance should you delay in sending your Form E to the court. Send the following cover letter:

"I file this Form E on the basis that the other side was not ready to exchange pursuant to the court order and I ask the court not to send a copy of my documents to the other side until they have filed theirs."

What happens next after I have sent Form E?
You should check the court order and see what needs to be done next in the court timetable.

You will have the opportunity to ask questions on your spouse's Form E.

Appendix

Appendix 1 – Form E (correct as of January 2023)

Financial statement

- For a financial order under the Matrimonial Causes Act 1973/ Civil Partnership Act 2004
- For financial relief after an overseas divorce etc under Part 3 of the Matrimonial and Family Proceedings Act 1984/Schedule 7 to the Civil Partnership Act 2004

To be completed by the relevant party	
Name of court	Case No.
Name of Applicant	
Name of Respondent	

of

(please tick appropriate boxes)

☐ Spouse ☐ Civil partner

Dated ☐☐/☐☐/☐☐☐☐

The parties are

_____ and _____

Who is the
- ☐ Spouse ☐ civil partner
- ☐ Petitioner ☐ Applicant ☐ Respondent in the
- ☐ divorce ☐ dissolution ☐ nullity
- ☐ (judicial) separation ☐ financial relief application

Applicant in this matter

Who is the
- ☐ Spouse ☐ civil partner
- ☐ Petitioner ☐ Applicant ☐ Respondent in the
- ☐ divorce ☐ dissolution ☐ nullity
- ☐ (judicial) separation ☐ financial relief application

Respondent in this matter

This form should only be completed in applications for a financial order (which can only be applied for as part of a divorce, dissolution, annulment or (judicial) separation in the High Court or family courts in England and Wales) or for applications for financial relief after an overseas divorce/dissolution etc. If the application is for any other financial remedy please complete Form E1.

This form should be used if the application is for the variation of an order for periodical payments where the applicant seeks the dismissal (immediate or otherwise) of the periodical payments order and its substitution with one or more of a lump sum order, a property adjustment order, a pension sharing order or a pension compensation sharing order. If you are making such an application, you must complete sections 1.14 and 5.1(e) of this form.

If the application is for any other variation of an order for a financial remedy please complete Form E2.

Please fill in this form fully and accurately. Where any box is not applicable, write 'N/A'.

You have a duty to the court to give a full, frank and clear disclosure of all your financial and other relevant circumstances.

A failure to give full and accurate disclosure may result in any order the court makes being set aside.

If you are found to have been deliberately untruthful, criminal proceedings may be brought against you for fraud under the Fraud Act 2006.

The information given in this form must be confirmed by a statement of truth. **Proceedings for contempt of court may be brought against a person who makes or causes to be made, a false statement in a document verified by a statement of truth.**

You must attach documents to the form where they are specifically sought and you may attach other documents where it is necessary to explain or clarify any of the information that you give.

Essential documents that must accompany this statement are detailed in the form.

If there is not enough room on the form for any particular piece of information, you may continue on an attached sheet of paper.

If you are in doubt about how to complete any part of this form you should seek legal advice.

This statement is filed by

| Solicitor's fee account no. | |

Name and address of solicitor

1 General Information

1.1 Full name

1.2 Date of birth | Date | Month | Year

1.3 Date of the marriage/civil partnership | Date | Month | Year

1.4 Occupation

1.5 Date of the separation | Date | Month | Year | Tick here if not applicable ☐

1.6 Date of the

Petition for divorce/dissolution/nullity/(judicial) separation			Decree nisi/conditional order/(judicial) separation order			Decree absolute/final order (if applicable)		
Date	Month	Year	Date	Month	Year	Date	Month	Year

1.7 If you have subsequently married or formed a civil partnership, or will do so, state the date | Date | Month | Year

1.8 Are you living with a new partner? Yes ☐ No ☐

1.9 Do you intend to live with a new partner within the next six months? Yes ☐ No ☐

1.10 Details of any children of the family

Full names	Date of birth			With whom does the child live?
	Date	Month	Year	

1.11 Details of the state of health of yourself and the children if you think this should be taken into account

Yourself	Children

1.12 Details of the present and proposed future educational arrangements for the children.

Present arrangements	Future arrangements

1.13 Details of any child support maintenance calculation or any maintenance order or agreement made in respect of any children of the family. If no calculation, order or agreement has been made, give an estimate of the liability of the non-resident parent in respect of the children of the family under the Child Support Act 1991.

1.14 If this application is to vary an order, attach a copy of the order and give details of the part that is to be varied and the changes sought. You may need to continue on a separate sheet.

1.15 Details of any other court cases between you and your spouse/civil partner, whether in relation to money, property, children or anything else.

Case No	Court	Type of proceedings

1.16 Your present residence and the occupants of it and on what terms you occupy it (e.g. tenant, owner-occupier).

Address	Occupants	Terms of occupation

2 Financial Details

Part 1 Real Property (land and buildings) and Personal Assets

2.1 Complete this section in respect of the family home (the last family home occupied by you and your spouse/civil partner) if it remains unsold.

> Documentation required for attachment to this section:
> a) A copy of any valuation of the property obtained within the last six months. If you cannot provide this document, please give your own realistic estimate of the current market value
> b) A recent mortgage statement confirming the sum outstanding on **each** mortgage

Property name and address	
Land Registry title number	
Mortgage company name(s) and address(es) and account number(s)	
Type of mortgage	
Details of who owns the property and the extent of your legal and beneficial interest in it (i.e. state if it is owned by you solely or jointly owned with your spouse/civil partner or with others)	
If you consider that the legal ownership as recorded at the Land Registry does not reflect the true position, state why	
Current market value of the property	
Balance(s) outstanding on any mortgage(s)	
If a sale at this stage would result in penalties payable under the mortgage, state amount	
Estimate the costs of sale of the property	
Total equity in the property (i.e. market value less outstanding mortgage(s), penalties if any and the costs of sale)	

TOTAL value of your interest in the family home: Total A £

2.2 Details of your interest in any other property, land or buildings. Complete one page for each property you have an interest in.

> Documentation required for attachment to this section:
> a) A copy of any valuation of the property obtained within the last six months. If you cannot provide this document, please give your own realistic estimate of the current market value
> b) A recent mortgage statement confirming the sum outstanding on **each** mortgage

Property name and address	
Land Registry title number	
Mortgage company name(s) and address(es) and account number(s)	
Type of mortgage	
Details of who owns the property and the extent of your legal and beneficial interest in it (i.e. state if it is owned by you solely or jointly owned with your spouse/civil partner or with others)	
If you consider that the legal ownership as recorded at the Land Registry does not reflect the true position, state why	
Current market value of the property	
Balance outstanding on any mortgage(s)	
If a sale at this stage would result in penalties payable under the mortgage, state amount	
Estimate the costs of sale of the property	
Total equity in the property (i.e. market value less outstanding mortgage(s), penalties if any and the costs of sale)	
Total value of your interest in this property	

TOTAL value of your interest in ALL other property: Total B £

2.3 Details of all personal bank, building society and National Savings Accounts that you hold or have held at any time in the last twelve months and which are or were either in your own name or in which you have or have had any interest. This applies whether any such account is in credit or in debit. For joint accounts give your interest and the name of the other account holder. If the account is overdrawn, show a minus figure.

> Documentation required for attachment to this section:
> For each account listed, all statements covering the last 12 months.

Name of bank or building society, including branch name	Type of account (e.g. current)	Account number	Name of other account holder (if applicable)	Balance at the date of this statement	Total current value of your interest

TOTAL value of your interest in ALL accounts: (C1) £

2.4 Details of all investments, including shares, PEPs, ISAs, TESSAs, National Savings Investments (other than already shown above), bonds, stocks, unit trusts, investment trusts, gilts and other quoted securities that you hold or have an interest in. (Do not include dividend income as this will be dealt with separately later on.)

> Documentation required for attachment to this section:
> Latest statement or dividend counterfoil relating to each investment.

Name	Type of Investment	Size of Holding	Current value	Name of any other account holder (if applicable)	Total current value of your interest

TOTAL value of your interest in ALL holdings: (C2) £

2.5 Details of all life insurance policies including endowment policies that you hold or have an interest in. Include those that do not have a surrender value. Complete one page for each policy.

> Documentation required for attachment to this section:
> A surrender valuation of each policy that has a surrender value.

Name of company	
Policy type	
Policy number	
If policy is assigned, state in whose favour and amount of charge	
Name of any other owner and the extent of your interest in the policy	
Maturity date (if applicable)	Date / Month / Year
Current surrender value (if applicable)	
If policy includes life insurance, the amount of the insurance and the name of the person whose life is insured	
Total current surrender value of your interest in this policy	

TOTAL value of your interest in ALL policies: (C3) £ _____

2.6 Details of all monies that are OWED TO YOU. Do not include sums owed in director's or partnership accounts which should be included at section 2.11.

Brief description of money owed and by whom	Balance outstanding	Total current value of your interest

TOTAL value of your interest in ALL debts owed to you: (C4) £ _____

2.7 Details of all cash sums held in excess of £500. You must state where it is held and the currency it is held in.

Where held	Amount	Currency	Total current value of your interest

TOTAL value of your interest in ALL cash sums: (C5)	£

2.8 Details of personal belongings individually worth more than £500.
   INCLUDE:
   - Cars (gross value)
   - Collections, pictures and jewellery
   - Furniture and house contents

Brief description of item	Total current value of your interest

TOTAL value of your interest in ALL personal belongings: (C6)	£
Add together all the figures in boxes C1 to C6 to give the TOTAL current value of your interest in personal assets: TOTAL C	£

2 Financial Details   Part 2 Capital: Liabilities and Capital Gains Tax

2.9 Details of any liabilities you have.

EXCLUDE liabilities already shown such as:
- Mortgages
- Any overdrawn bank, building society or National Savings accounts

INCLUDE:
- Money owed on credit cards and store cards
- Bank loans
- Hire purchase agreements

List all credit and store cards held including those with a nil or positive balance. Where the liability is not solely your own, give the name(s) of the other account holder(s) and the amount of your share of the liability.

Liability	Name(s) of other account holder(s) (if applicable)	Total liability	Total current value of your interest in the liability

TOTAL value of your interest in ALL liabilities: (D1) £

2.10 If any Capital Gains Tax would be payable on the disposal now of any of your real property or personal assets, give your estimate of the tax liability.

Asset	Total Capital Gains Tax liability

TOTAL value of ALL your potential Capital Gains Tax liabilities: (D2) £

Add together D1 and D2 to give the TOTAL value of your liabilities: TOTAL D £

2 Financial Details — Part 3 Capital: Business assets and directorships

2.11 Details of all your business interests. Complete one page for each business you have an interest in.

> Documentation required for attachment to this section:
> a) Copies of the business accounts for the last two financial years
> b) Any documentation, if available at this stage, upon which you have based your estimate of the current value of your interest in this business, for example a letter from an accountant or a formal valuation.
> It is not essential to obtain a formal valuation at this stage

Name of the business	
Briefly describe the nature of the business	
Are you (please tick appropriate box)	☐ Sole trader ☐ Partner in a partnership with others ☐ Shareholder in a limited company
If you are a partner or a shareholder, state the extent of your interest in the business (i.e. partnership share or the extent of your shareholding compared to the overall shares issued)	
State when your next set of accounts will be available	
If any of the figures in the last accounts are not an accurate reflection of the current position, state why. For example, if there has been a material change since the last accounts, or if the valuations of the assets are not a true reflection of their value (e.g. because property or other assets have not been re-valued in recent years or because they are shown at a book value)	
Total amount of any sums owed to you by the business by way of a director's loan account, partnership capital or current accounts or the like. Identify where these appear in the business accounts	
Your estimate of the current value of your business interest. Explain briefly the basis upon which you have reached that figure	
Your estimate of any Capital Gains Tax that would be payable if you were to dispose of your business now	
Net value of your interest in this business after any Capital Gains Tax liability	

TOTAL value of ALL your interests in business assets: **TOTAL E** £ ☐

2.12 List any directorships you hold or have held in the last 12 months (other than those already disclosed in Section 2.11).

2 Financial Details

Part 4 Capital: Pensions and Pension Protection Fund (PPF) Compensation

2.13 Give details of all your pension rights and all PPF compensation entitlements, including prospective entitlements. Complete a separate page for each pension or PPF compensation entitlement.

EXCLUDE:
- Basic State Pension

INCLUDE (complete a separate page for each one):
- Additional State Pension (SERPS and State Second Pension (S2P))
- Free Standing Additional Voluntary Contribution Schemes (FSAVC) separate from the scheme of your employer
- Membership of ALL pension plans or schemes
- PPF compensation entitlement for each scheme you were a member of which has transferred to PPF

Documentation required for attachment to this section:
a) A recent statement showing the cash equivalent (CE) provided by the trustees or managers of each pension arrangement; for the additional state pension, a valuation of these rights or for PPF a valuation of PPF compensation entitlement
b) If any valuation is not available, give the estimated date when it will be available and attach a copy of your letter to the pension company, administrators, or PPF Board from whom the information was sought and/or state the date on which an application for a valuation of an Additional State Pension was submitted to the Department of Work and Pensions

Name and address of pension arrangement or PPF Board			
Your National Insurance Number			
Number of pension arrangement or reference number or PPF compensation reference number			
Type of scheme e.g. occupational or personal, final salary, money purchase, additional state pension, PPF or other (if other, please give details)			
Date the CE, PPF compensation or additional state pension was calculated	Date	Month	Year
Is the pension in payment or drawdown? (please answer Yes or No)	☐ Yes ☐ No		
State the CE quotation, the additional state pension valuation or PPF valuation of those rights			
If the arrangement is an occupational pension arrangement that is paying reduced CEs, please quote what the CE would have been if not reduced. If this is not possible, please indicate if the CE quoted is a reduced CE			
Is the PPF compensation capped? (please answer Yes or No)	☐ Yes ☐ No		

TOTAL value of ALL your pension assets: TOTAL F £

2 Financial Details   Part 5 Capital: Other assets

2.14 Give details of any other assets not listed in Parts 1 to 4 above.

INCLUDE (the following list is not exhaustive):
- Any personal or business assets not yet disclosed
- Unrealisable assets
- Share option schemes, stating the estimated net sale proceeds of the shares if the options were capable of exercise now, and whether Capital Gains Tax or income tax would be payable
- Business expansion schemes
- Futures
- Commodities
- Trust interests (including interests under a discretionary trust), stating your estimate of the value of the interest and when it is likely to become realisable. If you say it will never be realisable, or has no value, give your reasons
- Any asset that is likely to be received in the foreseeable future
- Any asset held on your behalf by a third party
- Any asset not disclosed elsewhere on this form even if held outside England and Wales

You are reminded of your obligation to disclose all your financial assets and interests of ANY nature.

Type of asset	Value	Total NET value of your interest

TOTAL value of ALL your other assets: TOTAL G   £

2 Financial Details   Part 6 Income: Earned income from employment

2.15 Details of earned income from employment. Complete one page for each employment.

> Documentation required for attachment to this section:
> a) P60 for the last financial year (you should have received this from your employer shortly after the last 5th April)
> b) Your last three payslips
> c) Your last Form P11D if you have been issued with one

Name and address of your employer	
Job title and brief details of the type of work you do	
Hours worked per week in this employment	
How long have you been with this employer?	
Explain the basis of your income i.e. state whether it is based on an annual salary or an hourly rate of pay and whether it includes commissions or bonuses	
Gross income for the last financial year as shown on your P60	
Net income for the last financial year i.e. gross income less income tax and national insurance	
Average net income for the last three months i.e. total income less income tax and national insurance divided by three	
Briefly explain any other entries on the attached payslips other than basic income, income tax and national insurance	
If the payslips attached for the last three months are not an accurate reflection of your normal income briefly explain why	
Details and value of any bonuses or other occasional payments that you receive from this employment not otherwise already shown, including the basis upon which they are paid	
Details and value of any benefits in kind, perks or other remuneration received from this employer in the last year (e.g. provision of a car, payment of travel, accommodation, meal expenses, etc.)	
Your estimate of your net income from this employment for the next 12 months. If this differs significantly from your current income explain why in box 4.1.2	

Estimated TOTAL of ALL net earned income from employment for the next 12 months: TOTAL H £

2 Financial Details — Part 7 Income: Income from self-employment or partnership

2.16 You will have already given details of your business and provided the last two years accounts at section 2.11. Complete this section giving details of your income from your business. Complete one page for each business.

> Documentation required for attachment to this section:
> a) A copy of your last tax assessment or, if that is not available, a letter from your accountant confirming your tax liability
> b) If net income from the last financial year and estimated net income for the next 12 months is significantly different, a copy of management accounts for the period since your last account

Name of the business	
Date to which your last accounts were completed	
Your share of gross business profit from the last completed accounts	
Income tax and national insurance payable on your share of gross business profit above	
Net income for that year (using the two figures directly above, gross business profit less income tax and national insurance payable)	
Details and value of any benefits in kind, perks or other remuneration received from this business in the last year e.g. provision of a car, payment of travel, accommodation, meal expenses, etc.	
Amount of any regular monthly or other drawings that you take from this business	
If the estimated figure directly below is different from the net income as at the end date of the last completed accounts, briefly explain the reason(s)	
Your estimate of your net annual income for the next 12 months	

Estimated TOTAL of ALL net income from self-employment or partnership for the next 12 months: TOTAL I £

2 Financial Details   Part 8 Income: Income from investments
e.g. dividends, interest or rental income

2.17 Details of income received in the last financial year (the year ended last 5th April), and your estimate of your income for the current financial year. Indicate whether the income was paid gross or net of income tax. You are not required to calculate any tax payable that may arise.

Nature of income and the asset from which it derived	Paid gross or net	Income received in the last financial year	Estimated income for the next 12 months

Estimated TOTAL investment income for the next 12 months: TOTAL J £

2 Financial Details

Part 9 Income: Income from state benefits (including state pension and child benefit)

2.18 Details of all state benefits that you are currently receiving.

Name of benefit	Amount paid	Frequency of payment	Estimated income for the next 12 months

Estimated TOTAL benefit income for the next 12 months: TOTAL K £

2 Financial Details   Part 10 Income: Any other income

2.19 Details of any other income not disclosed above.

INCLUDE:

Any source including a Pension (excluding State Pension), and Pension Protection Fund (PPF) compensation
- from which income has been received during the last 12 months (even if it has now ceased)
- from which income is likely to be received during the next 12 months

You are reminded of your obligation to give full disclosure of your financial circumstances

Nature of income	Paid gross or net	Income received in the last financial year	Estimated income for the next 12 months

Estimated TOTAL other income for the next 12 months: TOTAL L £

2 Financial Details   Summaries

2.20 Summary of your capital (Parts 1 to 5).

Description	Reference of the section on this statement	Value
Current value of your interest in the family home	A	
Current value of your interest in all other property	B	
Current value of your interest in personal assets	C	
Current value of your interest in business assets	E	
Current value of your pension and PPF compensation assets	F	
Current value of all your other assets	G	
Total value of your assets (Totals A+B+C+E+F+G)		£
Current value of your liabilities	D	
Value of your assets **LESS** the value of your liabilities (Totals A+B+C+E+F+G – D)		£

2.21 Summary of your estimated income for the next 12 months (Parts 6 to 10).

Description	Reference of the section on this statement	Value
Estimated net total of income from employment	H	
Estimated net total of income from self-employment or partnership	I	
Estimated net total of investment income	J	
Estimated state benefit receipts	K	
Estimated net total of all other income	L	
Estimated TOTAL income for the next 12 months (Totals H to L):		£

3 Financial Requirements   Part 1 Income needs

3.1 Income needs for yourself and for any children living with you or provided for by you. ALL figures should be annual, monthly or weekly (state which). You *must not* use a combination of these periods. State your current income needs and, if these are likely to change in the near future, explain the anticipated change and give an estimate of the future cost.

The income needs below are: (delete those not applicable)	☐ Weekly	☐ Monthly	☐ Annual
I anticipate my income needs are going to change because			

3.1.1 Income needs for yourself.

INCLUDE:
- All income needs for yourself
- Income needs for any children living with you or provided for by you only if these form part of your total income needs (e.g. housing, fuel, car expenses, holidays, etc)

Item	Current cost	Estimated future cost
SUB-TOTAL your income needs	£	

3.1.2 Income needs for children living with you or provided for by you.

INCLUDE:
- Only those income needs that are different to those of your household shown above

Item	Current cost	Estimated future cost
SUB-TOTAL children's income needs:	£	
TOTAL of ALL income needs:	£	

3 Financial Requirements   Part 2 Capital needs

3.2 Set out below the reasonable future capital needs for yourself and for any children living with you or provided for by you.

3.2.1 Capital needs for yourself.

INCLUDE:
- All capital needs for yourself
- Capital needs for any children living with you or provided for by you only if these form part of your total capital needs (e.g. housing, car, etc.)

Item	Cost
SUB-TOTAL your capital needs:	£

3.2.2 Capital needs for children living with you or provided for by you.

INCLUDE:
- Only those capital needs that are different to those of your household shown above

Item	Cost
SUB-TOTAL your children's capital needs	£
TOTAL of ALL capital needs:	£

4 Other Information

4.1 Details of any significant changes in your assets or income.

At both sections 4.1.1 and 4.1.2, INCLUDE:
- ALL assets held both within and outside England and Wales
- The disposal of any asset

4.1.1 Significant changes in assets or income during the LAST 12 months.

4.1.2 Significant changes in assets or income likely to occur during the NEXT 12 months.

4.2 Brief details of the standard of living enjoyed by you and your spouse/civil partner during the marriage/civil partnership.

4.3 Are there any particular contributions to the family property and assets or outgoings, or to family life, or the welfare of the family that have been made by you, your partner or anyone else that you think should be taken into account? If there are any such items, briefly describe the contribution and state the amount, when it was made and by whom.

INCLUDE:
- Contributions already made
- Contributions that will be made in the foreseeable future

4.4 Bad behaviour or conduct by the other party will only be taken into account in very exceptional circumstances when deciding how assets should be shared after divorce/dissolution. If you feel it should be taken into account in your case, identify the nature of the behaviour or conduct below.

4.5 Give details of any other circumstances that you consider could significantly affect the extent of the financial provision to be made by or for you or any child of the family.

INCLUDE (the following list is not exhaustive):
- Earning capacity
- Disability
- Inheritance prospects
- Redundancy
- Retirement
- Any agreement made between you and your spouse/civil partner before or after your marriage/civil partnership stating whether or not you rely upon the agreement giving your reasons
- Any plans to marry, form a civil partnership or live with a new partner
- Any contingent liabilities

4.6 If you have subsequently married or formed a civil partnership (or intend to) or are living with another person (or intend to), give brief details, so far as they are known to you, of his or her income, assets and liabilities.

Annual Income		Assets and Liabilities	
Nature of income	Value (if known, state whether gross or net)	Item	Value (if known)
Total income:	£	Total assets/liabilities:	£

5 Order Sought

5.1 If you are able at this stage, specify what kind of orders you are asking the court to make. Even if you cannot be specific at this stage, if you are able to do so, indicate:

   a) If the family home is still owned, whether you are asking for it to be transferred to yourself or your spouse/civil partner or whether you are saying it should be sold

   b) Whether you consider this is a case for continuing spousal maintenance/maintenance for your civil partner or whether you see the case as being appropriate for a 'clean break' *(A 'clean break' means a settlement or order which provides amongst other things, that neither you nor your spouse/civil partner will have any further claim against the income or capital of the other party. A 'clean break' does not terminate the responsibility of a parent to a child.)*

   c) Whether you are seeking a
      i) pension sharing order
      ii) pension attachment order
      iii) pension compensation sharing order
      iv) pension compensation attachment order

   d) If you are seeking a transfer or settlement of any property or assets, identify the property or assets in question

   e) Where you seek the dismissal, immediate or otherwise, of an order for periodical payments and its substitution with another order, whether the substituted order you seek is for
      i) a lump sum order
      ii) a property adjustment order
      iii) a pension sharing order and/or
      iv) a pension compensation sharing order.

5.2 If you are seeking a variation of an ante-nuptial or post-nuptial settlement or a relevant settlement made during, or in anticipation of, a civil partnership, identify the settlement, by whom it was made, its trustees and beneficiaries and state why you allege it is a settlement which the court can vary.

5.3 If you are seeking an avoidance of disposition order, or if you have already applied for such an order, identify the property to which the disposition relates and the person or body in whose favour the disposition is alleged to have been made.

Statement of Truth

*delete as appropriate

*[I believe] [the Applicant/Respondent believes] that the facts stated in this statement are true

*I am duly authorised by the Applicant/Respondent to sign this statement

and confirm that the information given above is a full, frank, clear and accurate disclosure of my financial and other relevant circumstances.

Print full name

Address for service

Postcode

Name of Applicant's/Respondent's solicitor's firm

Signed   Dated

*(Applicant/Respondent) (Litigation friend)
*(Applicant's/Respondent's solicitor)

Position or office held
(if signing on behalf of firm or company)

Proceedings for contempt of court may be brought against a person who makes or causes to be made, a false statement in a document verified by a statement of truth.

Address all communications to the Court Manager of the Court and quote the case number.
If you do not quote this number, your correspondence may be returned.

Schedule of Documents to accompany Form E

The following list shows the documents you must attach to your Form E if applicable. You may attach other documents where it is necessary to explain or clarify any of the information that you give in the Form E.

Form E paragraph	Document	Attached	Not applicable	To follow
1.14	**Application to vary an order:** if applicable, attach a copy of the relevant order.	☐	☐	☐
2.1	**Matrimonial home valuation:** a copy of any valuation relating to the matrimonial home that has been obtained in the last six months.	☐	☐	☐
2.1	**Matrimonial home mortgage(s):** a recent mortgage statement in respect of each mortgage on the matrimonial home confirming the amount outstanding.	☐	☐	☐
2.2	**Any other property:** a copy of any valuation relating to each other property disclosed that has been obtained in the last six months.	☐	☐	☐
2.2	**Any other property:** a recent mortgage statement in respect of each mortgage on each other property disclosed confirming the amount outstanding.	☐	☐	☐
2.3	**Personal bank, building society and National Savings accounts:** copies of statements for the last 12 months for each account that has been held in the last twelve months, either in your own name or in which you have or have had any interest.	☐	☐	☐
2.4	**Other investments:** the latest statement or dividend counterfoil relating to each investment as disclosed in paragraph 2.4.	☐	☐	☐
2.5	**Life insurance (including endowment) policies:** a surrender valuation for each policy that has a surrender value as disclosed under paragraph 2.5.	☐	☐	☐
2.11	**Business interests:** a copy of the business accounts for the last two financial years for each business interest disclosed.	☐	☐	☐
2.11	**Business interests:** any documentation that is available to confirm the estimate of the current value of the business, for example, a letter from an accountant or formal valuation if that has been obtained.	☐	☐	☐
2.13	**Pension and PPF compensation:** a recent statement showing the cash equivalent (CE) provided by the trustees or managers of each pension arrangement or valuation of each PPF entitlement provided by the PPF Board that you have disclosed (or, in the case of the additional state pension, a valuation of these rights). If not yet available, attach a copy of the letter sent to the pension company, administrators or the PPF Board requesting the information.	☐	☐	☐
2.15	**Employment income:** your P60 for the last financial year in respect of each employment that you have.	☐	☐	☐
2.15	**Employment income:** your last three payslips in respect of each employment that you have.	☐	☐	☐
2.15	**Employment income:** your last form P11D if you have been issued with one.	☐	☐	☐
2.16	**Self-employment or partnership income:** a copy of your last tax assessment or if that is not available, a letter from your accountant confirming your tax liability.	☐	☐	☐
2.16	**Self-employment or partnership income:** if net income from the last financial year and the estimated income for the next twelve months is significantly different, a copy of the management accounts for the period since your last accounts.	☐	☐	☐
State relevant Form E paragraph	Description of other documents attached:	☐	☐	☐

Appendix 2 – Schedule of outgoings

MONTHLY EXPENSE SCHEDULE

3.1. Please set out
- In the first column (a) your **current** expenditure for yourself (and children if any)
- In the second column (b) your anticipated reasonable future needs, so far as these are known.

The **second** column (b) should only be completed if your circumstances **are expected** to change, and may be **estimated** as far as necessary

If in doubt at this stage, leave column (b) blank for later **completion.**

Set out all your expenditure on a monthly basis for yourself and any children living with you.

Please do not mix annual, monthly and weekly figures

No.	Expenditure Item	(a) Current £	(b) Future £

No.	Expenditure Item	(a) Current £	(b) Future £
(A)	**Housing Costs**		
1.	Rent or mortgage payment		
2.	Ground Rent		
3.	Service Charge		
(A)	**Sub Total**		

No.	Expenditure Item	(a) Current £	(b) Future £
(B)	**Utilities/Maintenance Costs**		
4.	Council Tax		
5.	Water Rates		
6.	Electricity		
7.	Gas or oil		
8.	Telephone		
9.	Property & Household insurance		
10.	Home maintenance, cleaning and repair		
11.	Gardening costs		
(B)	**Sub Total**		

No.	Expenditure Item	(a) Current £	(b) Future £
(C)	**Financial Provision**		
12.	Pension provision		
13.	Life & endowment insurances		
14.	Repayment of debts (including HP)		
15.	Savings and investments		
16.	Boiler cover/appliance insurance or home emergency insurance		
	Sub Total		

(D)	**Miscellaneous**		
17.	Food		
18.	Day care/babysitting		
19.	Clothing		
20	School uniform		
21.	Tuition (if any)		
22.	Vehicle payments or leases		
23.	Vehicle insurance & license		
24.	Vehicle – petrol		
25.	Parking		
26.	Health Care: Insurance		
27.	Uninsured dental, orthodontic, medical, eye care		
28.	Work expenses & lunches		
29.	Entertainment expenses		
30.	Eating out & take-away		
31.	Sports & Leisure		
32.	School outings/trips		
33.	Books, music, video hire/purchase		
34.	Drinks & Tobacco		
35.	Holidays & breaks		
36.	Computer & Internet requisites		
37.	Membership fees & subscriptions		
38.	Charities & covenants		
39.	Gifts(birthdays, Christmas, etc)		
40.	Maintenance (other than children)		
41.	Other expenses (specify)		
(D)	**Sub Total**		

	Total monthly expenditure		
	X 12 = Total annual expenditure		

Signed:	
Dated:	

About the Author

Vinay Tanna DL is a solicitor and notary public at Garner & Hancock solicitors and has been in practice for 25 years. He is a managing director and now sits on various charity boards and provides advice, pro bono, to many organisations.

www.ingramcontent.com/pod-product-compliance
Lightning Source LLC
Chambersburg PA
CBHW042015090526
44587CB00027B/4267